Eat Sleep Wrestle

By John Cosper

Copyright 2014 by John Cosper

eatsleepwrestle.com
johncosper.com

Cover designed by Mike Simpson, Marked Out Photography. Back cover photo courtesy of Marked Out Photography.

Featured on the cover (left to right): Jamin Olivencia, Hy Zaya, "Crazy" Mary Dobson, Aaron Williams, Zodiak.

Back cover: Chris Hero (on the chair), Reed Bentley (under the chair.)

For Jason,
The one and only "Crybaby" Chris Alexander

Ron Mathis waits for another chop from Aaron Williams.
(Photo courtesy Michael Herm Photography.)

INTRODUCTION

New Albany, Indiana, is not the kind of place you normally associate with professional wrestling. It is the hometown of Rob Conway, a former WWE World Tag Team Champion and a two time NWA World Champion, but the little town located across the Ohio River from Louisville, Kentucky, is known primarily for two things: Harvest Homecoming, the second largest festival in the state after the Indy 500; and a rabid passion for high school basketball.

On July 5, 2014, shortly after Conway began his second reign as NWA Champ, a crowd of about a hundred people packed into the New Albany Production House and saw what would, on any card in any town, be considered the match of the night. "The Regulators" Aaron Williams and Ron Mathis took to the ring against Jake Crist and Alex Colon to defend the Destination One Wrestling Tag Team Championship belts. Williams and Mathis were the victors of a hard-fought battle with spectacular high spots and a flurry of false finishes, and when all was said and done, the crowd rose to its feet knowing that on this night, they had seen something special.

Williams, Mathis, Colon, and Crist are not household names. They don't have the marketing of WWE Superstars, and D1W, like most small promotions, can't come close to the spectacle the WWE creates. Nevertheless, the people in attendance that night came to see one thing: professional wrestling. They got all that and more with superb character work, storytelling, and lightning quick sequences with one move after another. The match encapsulated everything the wrestlers and fans loved about their sport, and fans were quick to get on their Twitter and Facebook accounts afterwards to let the rest of the world know what an amazing match they missed.

Nights like this, moments of glory that are seldom captured on film, happen all the time. They happen in warehouses, high school gyms, armories, flea markets, county fairs, roller rinks, backyards, civic centers, churches, and just about anywhere else you can cram a wrestling ring and some folding chairs.

Very few of the people who create these moments are full-time wrestlers. They are students, part-time and full-time employees who depend on other sources of income to get by. They sacrifice countless hours to sharpen their skills, develop their ring personas, to nurse injuries, and to drive to remote destinations for small crowds and low pay.

They don't do it for the money; this is all about passion, drive, and determination. These men are not superstars, and the ladies are certainly not divas. They are road warriors in the truest sense. They are professional wrestlers cut from the same cloth as Lou Thesz, Mildred Burke, and all those who traveled from city to city in the old territory days of wrestling. Yes, the old territory system is dead, but in the midst of the WWE era, a new one has arisen to take its place.

When I began my first book, *Bluegrass Brawlers*, in December of 2013, there were two promotions running in the Louisville area: the fledgling D1W, and Ohio Valley Wrestling, the former WWE territory that produced John Cena, Brock Lesnar, and Rob Conway. A year and a half later there were five. Underground Wrestling Alliance and Evolution Pro Wrestling both opened their doors for the first time, and Ian Rotten breathed new life into his legendary indie creation IWA Mid-South.

These new territories are smaller in scale than their predecessors, and the territories they occupy are much smaller. Nevertheless, they share much in common with the old days, including rivalries, in-fighting, and betrayals. More important, they all feature hungry, passionate workers desperate to hit it big.

Eat, Sleep, Wrestle will introduce you to today's indie wrestlers, the men and women keeping the sport and its traditions alive. You'll discover who they are, where they came from, how they got to where they are now, and what it's like to be an indie wrestler in today's system.

Independent wrestling is everywhere. It's in all fifty States, Canada, Mexico, Puerto Rico, Japan, Australia, Europe, and just about everywhere else you can imagine. Most of the wrestlers profiled in this book hail from the Midwestern United States, with some from the Northeast, Canada, and other regions. This book is not intended to be a complete survey of independent wrestling, but a glimpse into the life of those who are keeping the tradition alive. It's a chance for fans to walk in the shoes of the men and women who put their bodies on the line in the name not of sports entertainment, but wrestling. If your favorite promotion or wrestler is not included here, do not take it as a slight. This is just one small piece of the pie and a tribute to all who have stepped inside the squared circle.

Some of those whose stories appear in this book may no longer be active by the time you read this book. Some may be in new territories, trying out new gimmicks, and seeking new challenges. One or more may one day rise above the independents and make his mark on the grand stage of the WWE or one of the other major television promotions. A few have already caught the eye of the WWE, and one is already on the way to the Performance Center in Orlando.

Whatever they may or may not accomplish, no one can take away what they have done. Of all the millions of people who grow up as wrestling fans, they were the ones who went for it. They set their sights on a dream, and they gave it their all. They chose not to settle, but to see if they had what it takes in one of the most demanding, grueling businesses around.

They are not superstars. They are professional wrestlers. This is their story.

Jamin Olivencia with the OVW title.
(Photo courtesy Jamin Olivencia.)

"MOM, DAD, I WANT TO BE A WRESTLER"

From the age of 5, Jamin Olivencia wanted to be a professional wrestler. It was at that tender young age the Buffalo, New York, native discovered wrestling on television, and from that moment on, he could not think of anything else. When he wasn't watching wrestling on television, he was practicing moves. When he wasn't doing either, he was daydreaming about being in the ring.

Jamin didn't just daydream in front of the TV. He daydreamed everywhere, even at school. All those daydreams put him and his parents in an awkward situation at school one day.

"The school called my parents in," Jamin recalls. "They told them I needed to be in special ed. They said I was unresponsive in class. They wanted to get me tested. It turned out I didn't have any disabilities or anything. I was unresponsive because I was daydreaming about wrestling all the time!"

Every Mom and Dad has dreams for their child. Parents always hope and pray that their kids will grow up, find a good career, have a family, and do better than they did. So what's it like to go to your Mom and Dad and inform them that you've chosen a life of long drives, low pay offs, and almost chronic pain?

"I don't recall that conversation specifically," says Mike Quackenbush, the co-founder of CHIKARA Pro Wrestling. "But I'm sure as soon as it was over, and I left the room, they turned to each other and said something to the effect of, 'This is just a phase. He'll grow out of it, right?'"

Mike's parents weren't the only ones who didn't believe in the dream. "I remember at least one conversation with a high school guidance counselor who outright told me, 'You can't be that,' in reference to being a professional wrestler. It was if that idea was the most ludicrous thing she'd heard."

For most of the men and women profiled in this book, telling their parents wasn't a very dramatic moment. Most of their parents were not at all surprised by their children's choices because they saw them coming early on. As Ohio native Ron Mathis put it, "My parents said I came out of the womb watching wrestling."

Louisville, Kentucky native Austin WGS Bradley discovered wrestling at the age of five when his grandfather let him watch Nitro. Austin saw Chris Jericho versus Eddie Guerrero that night, and he got so into it, his grandfather pulled out a video camera to film his reaction.

"When I was eight, I told my parents I was going to be a wrestler," says Bradley. "They hoped it was a phase, but when I turned 18, they supported my decision."

Hy Zaya, a fellow Louisville native, didn't have to tell his parents. "I think they always knew," he says. "My father was a wrestler. Amateur, high school. He always had guys over to watch the big pay-per-views. I think the first match I remember seeing on TV was Hulk Hogan vs. Andre the Giant. My dad's mom loved wrestling too. She was a huge fan of the Moondogs."

Like many kids growing up in Louisville, Kentucky, Hy Zaya watched USWA wrestling on Wave 3. "I remember watching those guys work and hitting the mat," he says. "I remember thinking, man, that mat sounds hard!"

Wrestler J B Thunder lived down the street from Hy Zaya and was a favorite of the boys in the neighborhood. Thunder would take kids to the matches with him on occasion, but it was a long time before he gave in to Hy Zaya's pleas. Finally, one night, Thunder took the boy not to USWA at the Louisville Gardens, but to "The Mecca," the old Kmart building that once housed Ian Rotten's IWA Mid-South Wrestling, one of the most famous/infamous promotions of the last twenty years. It was Ian Rotten who first brought talented young stars like Chris Hero, Colt Cabana, and CM Punk to the public eye, but Rotten also enjoys a well-deserved reputation as the King of the Deathmatches.

"We got down there and got in line," says Hy Zaya. "I looked around, and my first impression was, 'Why am I standing here around all these white people with weapons?'"

Ian Rotten was also one of those kids who couldn't get enough wrestling. "To say we were obsessed would be an understatement," he says, referring to himself and his childhood best friend Mark Wolf. The former ECW talent and IWA Mid-South founder grew up in Baltimore, Maryland, a block up the street from his buddy Mark. "Mark's family had one of those giant satellite dishes. I'd walk down the block to his house at 8 am Saturday morning and wouldn't go home until 4 am, when Pacific Palisades Wrestling in Hawaii went off the air."

On Sundays, Mark would be at Ian's house by 9 am, playing a card and dice game they ordered out of the back of Pro Wrestling Illustrated. "We weren't satisfied with the cards that came with the game. Our moms took the cards to work and made copies of the cards so we could make our own. An Eddie Gilbert card became Bobby Fulton, and so on."

When their parents forced them to go outside, they played home run derby in the street. Rotten has always been an Oriole fan and a Cal Ripken, Jr., fan, but when the boys played baseball, their players were wrestlers. "Jerry Lawler was my go-to guy because he never lost."

Marc Hauss was one of the few to actually get into wrestling before leaving high school. He started with some backyard groups at the age of fifteen. "I was not allowed to watch it because they did not want me to follow in the footsteps of any wrestler and become one. I only first started watching it when I was 12 and became hooked."

Marc's parents weren't thrilled when he started training for real at the age of seventeen, but they backed off a little when he agreed to finish college, a step strongly recommended by many wrestling legends including Jim Cornette, Mick Foley, and Roddy Piper.

"Over the years they have softened on their stance and come to shows here and there," says Hauss, "But for the most part it is not their favorite thing that I am doing right now."

CZW alum and Ring of Honor star Adam Cole was one of those kids so obsessed with wrestling that wrestling T-shirts made up the majority of his wardrobe. He wore his favorite shirts so often, one of his classmates offered him twenty dollars if he would wear a different shirt for one day. "I took her money and used it to buy The Rock's 'Just Bring It' T-shirt with the American flag on it."

One of Cole's best friends had the chance to date a girl he really liked, but he had to find a date for the girl's best friend. He asked Cole to go on a double date, and Adam found himself matched with a very attractive girl. They took the girls to the mall, where Cole bought a WWE DVD, and went back to the house.

Cole put the new DVD on while his friend began making out with his girl. Cole's date wanted some action too, and during a heated match between Randy Orton and Rey Mysterio, she began kissing his neck to get his attention. Cole ignored her at first but finally turned and told her, "Listen, you're gonna have to stop until this match is over."

Cole missed out on the girl, but not his calling. When he was still in high school, he caught up with CZW owner DJ Hyde after a show and told him he planned to train when he turned eighteen. "Why not now?" Hyde asked him. To Cole's surprise, Hyde arranged for him to begin training on a limited basis while he was still in high school.

Hyde began watching at the age of five but got into the wrestling business later than most. He was a college graduate earning six figures at a nice bank job, when wrestling reached out to him. Hyde had been following several wrestling promotions up and down the east coast. He was known to a number of wrestlers, who began teaching him how to take bumps. Next thing he knew, he was in the ring filling in for a no-show.

"When I told my parents I was going to be a wrestler, they were like, 'All right, cool.' It was when I told them I was leaving the bank to go full-time they said, 'That's on you.'"

Montreal native LuFisto decided to give wrestling a try when a new school opened up in town. "I was told by a few that I was too fat, too small and that wrestling was not for girls, especially by my step-father and guys in the class.

"The reputation of wrestlers wasn't too good, especially for women, as many thought that women wrestling were mainly strippers fighting in bars. My mom was against it. She tried to convince me to give up, but when she saw I wouldn't, she actually helped me by paying for my classes. She's been telling me to quit ever since. Must be because she is a nurse!"

Cincinnati native Aaron Williams saw professional wrestling as a chance to combine two of his passions, wrestling and martial arts. When he told his father he was going to be a wrestler, his dad laughed. When his dad saw Aaron was serious, he encouraged his son, saying, "If you're going to do it, do it big, and do it the best you can."

"I had a cherry red Mustang convertible back then," says Williams. "I wasn't sure how I was going to pay for classes, but just as I was getting ready to sign up, I totaled the car. I collected the insurance money and used it to pay for training. It was a blessing in disguise."

Toronto native Cherry Bomb proudly credits her father as being her inspiration for becoming a wrestler. Cherry's parents divorced when she was young, and she lived with her mother, aunt, and cousins in her grandmother's house. She visited her father on weekends, and that's where her passion for wrestling began.

"Dad would turn on wrestling and say, 'This is Hulk Hogan. Watch him,'" she remembers. Her cousins never took to the sport like she did, but Cherry's father watched wrestling with her and took her to her first live matches. "When Shawn Michaels won the title at WrestleMania XII, I ran to the phone and called my Dad. I was at a friend's house, and he was watching with his buddies. We were both so excited, and we said we had to watch it again together."

After Cherry lost her father at the age of twelve, wrestling lost its appeal. She got into music and played in several bands, but it wasn't until late in her high school career that she began watching wrestling again.

That was when she discovered Trish Stratus. The women Cherry remembered from her childhood were managers like Sherri Martel and Sunny. Trish opened her mind to the possibility that women could wrestle. On career day in Grade 12 at her all girls Catholic high school, Cherry made a bulletin board covered in WWE Divas and told her classmates that they would all see her one day on the WWE.

Cherry wasn't the only wrestler to announce her intentions at career day. "The Blackanese Assassin" Menace did the same. "I listed two things that I wanted to do. Wrestling was number one on that list along with being a Kindergarten teacher. I remember the look on a lot of people's faces when I said a pro wrestler."

Menace began watching at a young age and grew up on Mid-Atlantic, Georgia Championship Wrestling, the WWF, and the NWA. "I always wanted to be a wrestler when I grew up. I don't think anybody in the family thought about it seriously, but it was always in my mind that, yes, I want to wrestle."

Fans may be surprised to know that deathmatch legend Mad Man Pondo grew up in a mostly quiet family. Pondo's grandparents were laid back, religious people, but when pro wrestling came on TV, something came over his grandmother, who would yell and scream and even cuss at the TV.

A man in Pondo's neighborhood named Roy West, Jr., took an active interest in Pondo and the other nearby kids. West told the kids if they kept their grades up, he would take them to wrestling. "All of a sudden, I became a straight A student," brags Pondo.

It's hard to imagine a guy like Mad Man Pondo before wrestling, telling his family that he was going to become a wrestler, but just about everyone went through it. Even Zodiak, another masked deathmatch specialist from Kentucky, had to run his decision by Mom.

"My mom actually took it rather well," he says. "She hasn't come to many events, but she has been supportive, yet protective, in that mom way. I had picked up some info about training from a booth at the Flea Market in Richwood, KY. They guy there gave me a number and when I told mom about it she just said, "Well, call them and see what it's about, but don't kill yourself."

Lylah Lodge never planned to become a wrestler. It was her brother and his friends who created a backyard wrestling group and dreamed of going pro. When her brother and his friends decided to sign up for professional training, Delilah tailed along.

"I was very heavy-set," says Lylah, "Much, much more than I am now. I didn't look like an athlete, and I certainly didn't feel athletic. But when we walked into the training school, the owner saw me and immediately wanted to know if I was there to train."

The owner was wrestling legend "Playboy" Buddy Rose, who didn't see a "fat chick" but a young woman with real potential. At Buddy's insistence Lylah began to train with her brothers. She soon found she was more athletic than she realized, and the bumping that comes in professional wrestling came naturally to her. She continued her training with everyone who would teach her, including Davey Richards and Dave Hollenbeck, trying to pick up new things and master the art of ring psychology.

The only wrestler I spoke with whose mother flat out objected to his career choice was Apollo "Showtime" Garvin. Garvin knew darn well his mom would not approve of him entering the squared circle, so when it came time to make his move, he simply didn't tell her. "When she found out, she just shook her head. She's still not a fan of what I do, even after twenty years. But honestly, she was more upset about my first tattoo and my brief career as a male stripper than she ever was about wrestling."

One of the most inspiring stories is that of Michael Hayes. Hayes, who is not to be mistaken for Michael P.S. Hayes of the Freebirds, joined the Army right out of high school. On a tour of duty in Iraq, Hayes was severely wounded when the Humvee he was riding hit an IED. Hayes suffered severe burns over large portions of his body and lost his left leg.

After eighteen months of rehab at Brooke Army Medical Center, Hayes returned to his home town of Louisville, Kentucky. He enrolled in college and got a job, but he also began drinking heavily. He was well on his way to becoming another statistic, another wounded vet who could never put his life together.

That changed one day when Hayes met some students from nearby Ohio Valley Wrestling. The former WWE developmental territory was affiliated with TNA Wrestling at the time. More importantly, the teachers at OVW were not afraid to take on a challenge themselves in helping Michael learn to wrestle.

For many of the wrestlers profiled in these pages, becoming a wrestler was the fulfillment of a dream. For Hayes, it was a second chance, a chance to make something good out of something tragic. He went from wounded vet to becoming one of the top stars in the OVW territory.

But I'm getting ahead of myself, aren't I? Telling your family you're going to be a wrestler is just the first step on the road to glory. Many young men and women break the news to their parents every year. Only a small percentage of those parents actually have to go through the trauma of watching their baby wrestle over the long haul. That's not because places to train are hard to find. There are more options than ever today, and they're all glad to take your money. It's staying the course and sticking it out that separates the fans from the future stars.

Apollo "Showtime" Garvin ready to fight.
(Photo courtesy Michael Herm Photography.)

PAYING YOUR DUES

It's Tuesday night around 8 PM, and the entrepreneurs who run the New Albany Production House are locking up. Music lessons are in full swing in the practice rooms down the hall from their still under construction offices and state of the art recording studios. The day is nearly over on this side of the building, but in the adjacent warehouse, a handful of wrestling students are busy setting up a ring for their weekly training session.

Apollo "Showtime" Garvin is the man in charge tonight. As he watches his eager young trainees put together the metal frame of the wrestling ring, he shakes his head. "Whole different world," he says. "Way different than when I started."

Garvin started about twenty years earlier in one of the first groups of students to train at Danny Davis' Ohio Valley Wrestling. The old OVW training center was a mere ten minutes from the Production House in nearby Jeffersonville. Davis set up shop in the Quadrangle, an old military installation turned warehouse complex that was seemingly on its last legs. Like the Production House, the Quadrangle now stands as a symbol of urban renewal, transformed from a condemned property into a repurposed office and shopping complex.

In Garvin's time, however, the Quadrangle was a mess of bricks and cobwebs, a building with no air conditioning, no restroom, and zero creature comforts, but that is not the different world Garvin refers to.

"When I started at OVW, we trained in the ring. Just beyond the ring was the curtain that led backstage. No one in the beginner's class was allowed past the curtain. You had to earn it."

Time was when every aspiring wrestler entered the business the same way Garvin did. Wannabes were first admitted into the arena to help set up the ring, just like Garvin's students. If time allowed, a veteran would invite them into the ring to learn the ropes and take their lumps. It wasn't until long after that first time setting up the ring, long after they'd have their first match even, that the students were "smartened up" to the business.

The secrets of professional wrestling were laid bare long ago. Even though everyone accepts that wrestling is staged, students at OVW and other promotions are taught the same art that wrestlers have passed down from generation to generation: how to tell a story in the ring that will make the audience, no matter how "smart," suspend their disbelief.

Mitchell Huff, who trains at Destination One and wrestles as "The Chosen One," began training at OVW in 2007. "I was first trained by a guy named Mo. He was a wrestler from the Intermediate class. We trained two days a week for two hours. The beginning of training was very basic, learning how to bump and run the ropes. We also did a lot of Hindu squats and push ups to test people's will. Then, Tank Toland and Seth Skyfire took over our class. Those guys taught me ring psychology and so much more.

"The first time I ran the ropes, I was running them at full sprint. I came from the basketball world where the faster the better, so I was trying to really impress my teachers and ran as fast as I possibly could. I guess they wanted to teach me a lesson and didn't tell me to stop for about two and a half minutes of straight sprinting. I was so gassed, I had to sneak away from the class to the bathroom and throw up."

Mitchell excelled in his class and became the go-to guy for giving newcomers a tryout match in front of the class. "You see all kinds of guys come to the beginners class that have a dream, but you can usually tell pretty quickly who has a shot, and most do not. There was a kid in our class named Leo who was about 5'11 and 165 lbs. soaking wet with not an athletic bone in his body. After weeks and weeks of training he was not getting better. One day I was running a spot with Leo where I shot him off the ropes and was supposed to duck his clothesline. I shot him off and ducked. The next think I know I saw a little black. I raised up and my nose was splattered all over my face, pouring blood, because the amazingly athletic Leo somehow threw an uppercut as a clothesline."

Jamin Olivencia moved to Louisville, Kentucky and OVW for one reason. "If you wanted to make it to the WWE, you had to go to Louisville," says Jamin, who has been a top star in the promotion ever since. "The thing that surprised me the most about OVW was the conditioning. Not just cardio, but wrestling conditioning. Rip Rogers emphasized conditioning in all phases of wrestling. He'd have us do one hold for an hour and then switch. We'd work one part of the body, then another. The head, an arm, even a finger."

Rogers' emphasis on such conditioning allowed his students to develop muscle memory for every hold and every move used in the wrestling ring. OVW students don't have to stop and think through their actions in the ring. They've run the ropes and locked on the holds for literally hours. Even the Big Show, who was sent down from the main roster for training, spent hours running the ropes. Danny Davis has the bent ring posts to prove it. (Show had to buy Davis a new set!) Wrestling conditioning freed Rip's students to concentrate on telling a story and entertaining a crowd, making them better all-around performers.

When Cherry Bomb began her wrestling training in Toronto right after her eighteenth birthday, she brought a tag along: her mom. "My mom is my best friend," says Cherry, who insists it wasn't at all weird to have mom sitting there, keeping an eye out and cheering for her. "If anyone has a problem with my mom, then that's their problem!"

Zodiak began his training at Bonekrushers, the training school for the Northern Wrestling Federation, run by Roger Ruffen out of Cincinnati. "At the time Chris Parks/Abyss was also there helping a lot with training and whatever the school needed. This is also the same place that produced Chris Harris, Jillian Hall, and Karl Anderson. It was always great working with them. We trained three days a week when I started and had shows on the weekends, typically every Saturday, so literally all week was something involving the wrestling business. We went over everything: drills, basic moves, promos, weight training, cardio, and more.

"It was always interesting seeing all the people come and go. There was no air conditioning, so it was hot in the summer and cold in the winter. We were all required to help keep the gym clean, travel, set up and tear down the rings, do security, clean after shows and whatever else needed done. Looking back now, these things were so important in teaching respect and keeping guys humble. They are key to developing the right mindset."

Eric Emanon trained at the Tyger's Den in Upstate New York, a school that later became the training center for Next Era Wrestling. "I learned some hard lessons early on. I watched training classes come and go; only a few people from each class actually stuck with it. I also learned that you need to trust and have respect for whoever is across the ring from you. I suffered a concussion early on in my training due to another student from another school who felt he was bigger than the business. Luckily he disappeared a few years later."

Decades ago, the wannabes began by traveling with the crew, setting up the ring, carrying bags for the wrestlers, and taking a beating when no one else is around.

"In the old days, the older guys worked with the new guys and teach them as they go," remembers Rip Rogers. "They would tell the new guy, 'Tonight we're going to do a Sunset Flip. Do you know how to do a Sunset Flip? Okay, here's how.' They weren't really taking them under their wing, of course. They just didn't want to die at the hands of a guy who didn't know what he was doing!"

Only a handful of promoters offer anyone such an opportunity today. Ian Rotten of IWA Mid-South is one of them.

"I approached Ian at a show," says Rick Brady, now the co-owner of IWA Mid-South's rival promotion Destination One Wrestling. "I asked him how I could become a wrestler. Ian handed me fifty tickets for his next show and told me if I sold them all, he would train me."

Brady ended up buying most of the tickets himself and giving them away. He soon learned that training at Ian Rotten's IWA Mid-South was brutal and old school.

One of the more memorable exercises Rotten and others use is called "Chop Class." One student would stand against the ropes with their arms outstretched gripping the top rope. The other students would line up and take turns chopping the first student across the chest: ten chops with the right, ten chops with the left. If the student lasted through the entire line, they took their place in line and another student took their spot on the ropes. If the student let go of the ropes, even for a second, the line started over.

"You went home with bruises all across your chest and neck," recalls Apollo Garvin. "Burst blood vessels everywhere."

"I remember going home and soaking in an ice cold tub that night," says Rick Brady. "As much as it hurt, it felt so good to realize I made it."

To many veterans, Chop Class and other torturous drills are simply part of the process, part of "paying your dues." When LuFisto began training in Canada, she experienced more than her share of such treatment.

"Being the only girl wrestling in my province for a while, I got punched real hard in the face and stretched just to see if I was tough and would last. Most of the wrestlers' wives hated me because they thought I was there to steal their husband when I never gave a damn about them. They would start rumors just to make me quit. There was even a guy in one promotion that did everything he could to make me quit. He even said he wished I would commit suicide.

"There were no other girls training, so I had to wrestle the guys. I broke my wrist on my fourth match, but that didn't stop me. I wrestled with my cast. The first years were tough physically, but mostly mentally. No money, sleeping in a car or on a floor, setting up rings, working through injuries just so people wouldn't call me a crybaby or remind me again that 'wrestling wasn't for girls.' Thinking about it now, I don't know how I was to endure it all."

"Crazy" Mary Dobson, a young high flyer who in three years has traveled the world, began her training journey on MySpace. Dobson got into wrestling watching with her grandma, and she was a big fan of Mad Man Pondo. After friending him online, she got up the courage to ask him how she could train to be a wrestler.

Pondo told Mary to look up Mickie Knuckles, an IWA Mid-South veteran and one of the fiercest women wrestlers on the independent circuit. When Mickie responded, she asked Mary how difficult it might be to get to Charlestown, Indiana. "I replied back and told her, 'I live in Charlestown, Indiana!'"

After training with Mickie and Pondo for a year, Mary was offered a chance to go to the Kaientai Dojo in Japan, run by former WWE tag team star Taka Michinoku. She lived in the dojo with other trainees, and they trained from 10 am to 3 pm in the traditional Japanese style. The trainees took a three hour break before doing lucha training from six to nine at night with the Mexican wrestlers staying at the Dojo.

As for Mickie Knuckles, her training happened on the job at IWA Mid-South, where she learned to take bumps from Chris Hero, Bull Pain, Tracy Smothers, and many others. "I learned to grow thicker skin and keep my mouth shut and eyes and ears open."

Mickie did plenty of dirty jobs while she was in training, jobs that taught her to be humble. "I cleaned the locker rooms, piss buckets, the trash left over from the shows, put up and took down the ring, drove the ring truck, put up concessions, put up gimmicks, sold both concessions and gimmicks, ran sound, did security, managed, referee. You name it, I did it but it was all a part of paying dues."

Tyson Dux worked as a janitor at his wrestling school, the price he paid not only to attend classes, but to live at the school. "I never saw a dime. I was told to be at their beck and call. I almost starved to death, losing forty pounds and looking like death. As if that wasn't enough, I was told to shave my head and eye brows because it was funny."

Dux chose the school, billed as the Hart Brothers wrestling school, because it bore the biggest name in Canadian wrestling. Stu Hart had a hand in training the biggest names to come out of Canada in the latter half of the twentieth century, including his sons Bret and Owen. "I saw Smith Hart once the entire time I was there," he says. "He never got in the ring. We were totally grifted."

Mad Man Pondo endured a great deal of physical pain in his training. "I signed up with my buddy Slick. The guys who trained us didn't want any of us in the class to become wrestlers. They beat us down, day after day. When Slick finally quit, the abuse was even worse for me. It wasn't until a new class started that they finally let up and accepted me. They moved on to beat up the new guys."

Menace credits his ex-girlfriend with helping him find out where he could be trained. "My girlfriend at the time ran into a guy that she went to school with. They started catching up and out of the blue, he tells her that was training and was gonna be in a Battle Royal that weekend. She then asked if his trainer Rick Connors was looking for anymore trainees. He told us to come to the show because Rick would be there. We drove down that weekend to find Rick Connors. After the show, the friend introduced me to Rick, and I told him I wanted to be a wrestler. We exchanged numbers, and the very next day I was in Rick Connors back yard beginning my wrestling training.

"I hated my first two classes. I did forward rolls in his backyard. I'm thinking, 'OK this is gonna be like *The Karate Kid.* Wax on, wax off.' Week two was the same thing. I went up to Rick and said, 'This isn't training! I can do rolls in my own backyard and save my gas money!' Rick looked at me and said, 'OK.' He came to me and talked to me about locking up. He then showed me how and it all began."

After graduating high school, Reed Bentley accepted an academic scholarship to the University of Louisville. Bentley was a brilliant student who scored a 33 on the ACT test. He took pre-law and pre-med courses and did well, but the whole time, he was thinking about wrestling.

Like Menace, Bentley got his break at a store. He was working for Sam's Club when a co-worker told him her boyfriend was a wrestler. The boyfriend also worked at Sam's, and Reed soon came in contact with Livewire Championship Wrestling, a backyard group working in KY.

"I paid $150 for three months of training," says Bentley. "Basically, all I got for my money was access to the ring."

Bentley didn't even have the ring at first. Kentucky requires anyone who steps into a ring to have a license, and Bentley did not yet have one. Bentley had a background in Tae Kwon Do and Brazilian Jiu Jitsu that made him a natural at taking bumps, but those early bumps were taken on the hard barn floor outside the ring.

Hy Zaya's first venture in wrestling also happened as part of a backyard group. "It's not something I talk about much," he says. "But we weren't like most backyard guys. We didn't go for blood and stuff. We did wrestling."

Hy Zaya and his friends rented a ring from Ian Rotten. Some of Rotten's crew assisted the kids, who were all underage, with the ring set up and even provided a little "training." Once the ring was set up, vets like Harry Palmer and Cash Flo would take the teens in the ring and practice on them, letting the young wannabes pay their dues while they kept their skills sharp.

DJ Hyde broke in through Combat Zone Wrestling, a promotion he now owns. CZW had no formal training program at the time when Hyde started taking bumps, but Hyde has since trained hundreds of wrestlers through the school he started, and his methods are as old school as they get.

"Our tryout is bull—-," says Hyde. "When you come in for a tryout, my goal is to run you into the ground, until you can't go anymore. If you come back the next day, then you pass."

Adam Cole is one of the proud few to make it through the CZW school. "The first two or three months, training would be two hours wearing us down, trying to make us throw up. He used to make us do bumps on the concrete floor. At the time you're thinking, 'This is how all wrestling schools are,' so I didn't question it. I just kept on taking it, saying, 'Yes, sir, may I have another?'"

Hyde's methods paid off for Cole. Not only did he become a star in Ring of Honor and Pro Wrestling Guerrilla, he's caught the eye of WWE. "DJ always encouraged us to train everywhere we can with whomever we can, to always keep learning."

Not every trainer gives that advice, to study with everyone they can. Many of them want to keep their students (and their money) in house. But for those who truly want to excel, the training never ends. Wrestling styles vary by region, by country, and by era, and wrestlers are constantly seeking to learn from each other as well as the past.

During the heyday of IWA Mid-South in Charlestown, Indiana, Ian Rotten lived in a narrow trailer with his family, a huge VHS wrestling library, and whatever young stars needed a place to crash. CM Punk and Colt Cabana were two of the many who availed themselves of the lodging and the video collection.

"Those guys would sit up all night watching old tapes," Rotten says. "I'd go to bed at 1 AM, and when I got up at seven, they'd still be awake watching videos!"

Punk and Cabana loved to watch their own matches, looking for ways to improve. "They'd put on these tremendous matches, and when they watched themselves on video, they tore themselves apart. They were their own worst critics."

It's not uncommon for a class of twenty wrestlers to dwindle down to one. Training is designed to break you. It's designed to weed out those who don't want to put in the work. As cruel and senseless as some training regimens may seem to an outsider, they really do prepare dedicated students for life on the pro wrestling circuit. It's an achievement to come back the second day. It's a greater achievement to make it to the end of a training program. The reward for doing so is what every wannabe dreams of, a real match with a real audience.

One gauntlet ends, and another begins.

FIRST MATCH

When the WWE debuts a new wrestler, they pull out all the stops to make sure that new face makes a splash. One of the most memorable debuts came back in 2002 when Kurt Angle issued an open challenge to anyone in the locker room. A ripped, fresh-faced kid in red and black trucks and a crew cut stormed down to the ring, ready for action. When Angle asked what gave the new wrestler the nerve to come to the ring, John Cena responded, "RUTHLESS AGGRESSION!"

Cena put on a valiant fight before losing his first televised match. Later that evening he received a televised handshake from the big dog of the locker room, The Undertaker. A star was born.

That first televised confrontation with Angle was not Cena's first match. Cena had countless matches prior to his national debut at Ohio Valley Wrestling and other promotions. In reality a wrestler's first match is hardly ever a grand affair.

Students at OVW usually had their debut in a battle royal, where they would face Rip Rogers' version of Chop Class, "Chop Around the Clock." Fans would draw the names of wrestlers to appear in the match, but the drawings were rigged so the new guys would end up in the ring with veterans like Rip Rogers and Flash Flanagan. Once in the ring, the vets would christen the rookies by passing them around the ring and chopping the newbie as hard as they could in each of the four corners.

"I remember one kid getting passed to me," recalls Chris Alexander, one of OVW's early students. "His chest was beet red, and he was begging me, 'Please toss me over the top rope!' I told him, 'I'm sorry. If I toss you out, they're going to do it to me.' I chopped him and sent him to the next corner."

Austin Bradley's first real match at OVW was against Miles Pentecost. Austin and Miles practiced their match over and over, but the night of the show, Austin was very nervous. As he waited at the Bolin position behind the curtain (named for legendary OVW manager Kenny Bolin), Rip Rogers came up behind him.

"Are you nervous?" asked Rip.

"Yes," said Austin.

Rip grabbed Austin's butt and held on tight. Austin started to yell at his trainer. "What are you doing? Let go!"

Rip only grinned. "You like that, son? Huh? Does that make you excited?"

"Get off me!" Austin repeated.

Rip let go and started to walk away. He turned, and said, "You ain't nervous now, are you?"

Mitchell Huff wrestled his first match for OVW against another new wrestler, Atlas DaBone. "There was one mess up in the match. I dove off the top rope for a cross body. He was supposed to catch me and hit me with a back breaker. For some reason he didn't catch me and we both went down."

Huff panicked at first, but he quickly called another spot to get them back on track. "I remember thinking about the mistake and how bad it must have looked, but when we watched the match, it didn't look bad it all. It just looked like a bad ass flying cross body. I took from that, even if you mess up, it's not always as bad as it seems."

Mitchell learned another lesson following the match when the WWE's Dr. Tom Pritchard spoke to him and Atlas. Mitchell earned praise for his dropkicks and calling a solid match, but it was Atlas who got the most attention. "Rich had such a great look, and I realized how important a look was to make it in this business. Rich had a WWE contract within 6 months."

LuFisto's first match proved to be as challenging and educational as the training she endured. "Just before my entrance, some wrestlers spit on me and threw water at me saying, 'You'll never last.'

"My first opponent, a girl known as Sophie The Queen decided to change the whole match while we were wrestling. When I was calling her spots that were originally planned she would block the shot just saying, 'No!' The match turned out okay considering the situation although the finish looked like crap since she didn't want to take any big moves. I just planted her head in the mat and that was it.

"I can say I learned very early that anything can happen and you have to deal with the situation to the best of your abilities, all this by staying professional at all cost despite your anger."

Zodiak had a much different experience than LuFisto when he faced Dirty Chris Hayes at Peels Palace in Erlanger, Kentucky. "It was a very basic match in front of what at the time was the Northern Wrestling Federation's biggest venue. There were about 500 people there. It was a great time and feeling. I learned to keep things simple, breathe and relax and listen that night. Hayes took great care of me and we went on to have several matches that year around Kentucky."

Not everyone gets the opportunity to prepare themselves for their first match. Some in-ring debuts happen by surprise. If someone no-shows at an event, a trainee can find himself thrust into the spotlight, as DJ Hyde did when he found himself in the ring with Killer Kowalski, Jr.

"The Blackanese Assassin" Menace found himself at a similar situation when he went to a show with his trainer, Rick Connors. "An hour and half before the show Rick tells me and my training partners that we are gonna have a match that night. My first thought was 'Holy Crap!!!' I wasn't ready to make my in ring debut. I had no gear whatsoever and at this point we had been inside of a ring maybe four or five times.

"I went home to find something that I thought would pass for the night. I wore black workout pants, a white shirt with a ying yang on it, and a pair of black and white Nikes. I was a nervous wreck.

"That night we opened the show with a six man tag match. While on the apron waiting, I was a mess, but when I was tagged in it was like someone flipped the switch. I did the same things we did in practice. At one point in the match I did a dropkick. It must have been something special because that was the move of the match that everyone talked about. I remember the crowd going nuts when I did it."

Jamin Olivencia's first match at Empire State Wrestling was against Cade Cassidy. It was a squash match, like most early matches are, but it was an affirming experience for the young man who had always dreamed of wrestling. His energy and enthusiasm enabled him to make a connection with the crowd even though they had never seen him before. That's a near impossible task for a brand new babyface, but Olivencia's energy proved to be contagious. He's a natural babyface, and he makes that same instant connection with fans everywhere he goes.

Aaron Williams came into wrestling with a background in martial arts, but he was saddled with a very uncomfortable gimmick for his first match. "The promoter wanted me to be a collegiate wrestler, like Rick Steiner. He made me wear the headgear and everything. It was the complete opposite of who I was, and very uncomfortable."

Williams was happy to have the support of his family that night, as his mom, dad, and grandmother were in attendance. "My grandmother is a very sweet, Christian lady. It was funny to hear her screaming and yelling at my opponent."

Reed Bentley had two matches his first night in the ring. The first was a reverse battle royal, a match made famous by TNA Wrestling. Later that night he participated in a three way match, a match that he won. "I didn't get broken in right, so when I go out, I'm not going out on my back either!"

The most important thing most wrestlers recall about their first match is how affirming it was to finally be in the ring. Eric Emanon first appeared in a tag team match for Next Era Wrestling. "For our first match, it wasn't awful. It was kept super simple to give us the feel of how things felt at 'real time' with an audience. I knew after that, I had made the right choice and here we are 10 years later!"

Marc Hauss had a similar feeling after his first match. "It was a Battle Royal at a now defunct company called Roc City Wrestling. It was what it was and at the time I thought it was WrestleMania. After the match, I knew that this is what I wanted to do, and all it did was motivate me to get back in the ring."

Tyson Dux's first match was with his good friend and training partner Campbell Thompson. "It was horrible if you look at it from this time in my career now, but I came away from it knowing that I made it. I survived all the dues and bruises and aches and mental abuse. I was now a wrestler."

A wrestler's first match is a rite of passage, a moment of affirmation that they made the right choice in choosing to be a wrestler. Most wrestlers can tell you the date, the venue, and their opponent from their first match, even if they can't remember anything else.

"My first match was on August 2, 2003, against Hailey Hatred," says Mickie Knuckles. "I became knocked out and don't remember a thing. But my trainers said I went into auto pilot and then I knew that I loved it."

Hy Zaya, Gary Jay, John Wayne Murdoch, and Ian Rotten.
(Photo courtesy Marked Out Photography.)

GETTING OVER

In the early days of professional wrestling, most wrestlers looked alike. They were barrel-chested with short-cropped hair in small trunks. A few wore masks, some took on assumed names, but all portrayed themselves as athletes first.

Then came Gorgeous George.

Gorgeous George changed the face of professional wrestling. He was an athlete, but he was also larger than life. He had flowing blonde hair, flashy robes, and an assistant to carry his things, including a large vanity mirror, to the ring. Gorgeous George had charisma to go with the look. He was a larger than life figure. He was an attraction.

George was an abomination to the purists in the wrestling business, but the more tickets Gorgeous George sold, the more it became clear he was the future of the business. Today, anyone who wants to make it in professional wrestling has to have a character. The right character with the right talent can make all the difference for an aspiring wrestler. A bad character can put you on the fast track out of the business!

In his early days Chris Hero usually billed himself as the Wifebeater. The origins of the name are much more innocent than you might think. Hero used to wear the white tank tops dubbed as "wifebeaters" in high school, and he carried that over to his early wrestling days. The name earned Hero national attention after he was billed on a show in Platteville, Wisconsin. When a women's group objected to seeing a man named Wifebeater on all the posters for the upcoming wrestling show, the story went out on the Associated Press wire. Bill Maher discussed the Wifebeater on his show *Politically Incorrect*, and Jesse Ventura addressed the character on CNN.

Hero had some defenders in the media, who were quick to point out that a name is just a name. Jake "The Snake" Roberts is not actually a snake, after all, and Bret "Hitman" Hart did not actually kill people for money. Even so, the Wifebeater name was eventually dropped, and a hero was born. "I'm not just Chris Hero, I'm your hero!"

Eric Emanon, who bills himself as "The Punk Rock Prodigy," understands just how important it is to have a stand out character. "My ring persona is something that is me turned up to 15. It has to be. The Punk Rock Prodigy hailing from Los Angeles, California. It's all the things I can think that you could love and also hate about a California kid. As for my ring attire, it's something that I just feel represents me. The teal/blue and black color combo are something you don't see much now, especially in Upstate New York. I'm just trying to stand out and stay ahead of the game. That's why a lot of the t-shirts I sell and the jackets and vests I wear are something you won't see anywhere else because of the way I patch them and design them. It's all about being a game changer."

One way to be a game changer is to wear a mask. Masks create an aura of mystery about a character. They can also help an otherwise average looking wrestler establish a greater presence with the fans.

Menace isn't the biggest guy in independent wrestling, in height or bulk. He's a high flyer who used his skills on the ropes to build a reputation, but he wanted to go even further.

"I became Menace to try and make myself more profitable," he says about becoming the masked character. "My style was different from anything else on the scene. I am a huge fan of Japanese wrestling, and I have a background in Kempo Ju-Jitsu. I wanted to put those elements into my Menace character. I was dubbed 'The Blackanese Assassin' by John House when I went to work for CZW in Philadelphia. My mask is somewhat alike to

Hayabusa, a wrestler from Japan, and my character hails from the Land of the Rising Sun."

Zodiak picked up a mask at the request of NWF promoter Roger Ruffen. "We were at the Cincinnati Gardens doing a show in cooperation with the Mighty Ducks hockey team, and I was told to bring my gear and a mask. I had no idea what I was doing. Roger told me I would be wrestling in the mask as The Zodiak. I had no clue what to do! For some reason I immediately thought of the creepy way the Repo Man would walk around and move and went with that. It was a fun solid match against a man named Dozer, a big man and vet in the NWF. My original gear was black and red and I just kept that theme. It fit so I figured why change it.

Over time, the masked Zodiak has changed. "Zodiak evolved from being a simple masked assassin to a darker monk-style character to the horror movie character he is now. The development has been fun and fans seem to really enjoy it."

Change is essential for a wrestler to keep himself or herself current and original. Lylah Lodge's character has evolved in several ways during her years in the ring. "I adopted the name Delilah because I used to wrestle only men," she says. "I was a man killer, and Delilah fit the image."

Over time, the Delilah character evolved into a princess, a spoiled little rich girl type. "As manly as I know I am, I always try to be dainty and princessy. I adopted the tiara early on."

At OVW Al Snow helped Lylah to develop a backstory for the character. He put Lylah in the "Miss OVW" tournament, where Delilah morphed into more of a blushing dame. Her character became self-conscious, shy, uncertain of her own talents. "It was a lot like that movie *She's All That*," says Lylah. As the tournament went on, Lylah's confidence grew. So did the cheers when she took to the ring. By the time she faced Taelor Hendrix for the

Women's Championship, she had won over the OVW faithful.

Today, Lylah wrestles as Lylah and Delilah, depending on whatever a promoter is looking for. She also wrestles as May Belle Smothers, the kayfabe niece of Tracy Smothers, when she travels with the veteran.

Lylah's not alone in working both heel and babyface personas. Apollo "Showtime" Garvin frequently works as a heel and a babyface in the same weekend. One one side of the Ohio River, he's one of the most hated men, while on the south side he's one of the top babyfaces. "It confuses the fans a little," he admits. "Sometimes they're not sure if they should cheer me or boo me."

The confusion isn't restricted to the fans either. "I'll catch myself in the ring about to rip on someone in the crowd, and I'll remember, oh yeah, I can't say that tonight."

Colt Cabana is a natural babyface, and staying a babyface is vital to his financial success. People buy more merchandise from babyfaces, and Colt sells a lot of T-shirts. Nevertheless, Colt's success on the independent level has given him the leeway to play a tongue in cheek heel when he has to. His actions in the ring are pure heel, but they are done with a wink and a smile. When the show is over, the fans still know he's good old Colt Cabana.

LuFisto has been in the wrestling business a long time, and her ring character has continually evolved. Originally billed as "Precious Lucy," her signature name came to be thanks to a trip to Japan. "The name LuFisto comes from the mix of my old name 'Precious Lucy,' Mephisto from Batman, and Jedi Knight Kit Fisto from Star Wars. When I went to Japan, I was told that I couldn't use the name Lucy because Daffney had been there as Lucy Furr. Also, it was very hard for them to pronounce Precious. Therefore, I put together Lucy and Fisto: LuFisto. It's easy to remember, easy to pronounce in any language and sounds like something out of a comic book."

LuFisto's character was greatly inspired by the Manga and Anime she found in Japan. "I really liked their paradox: extreme cuteness juxtaposed with ultra-violence. I thought it was the perfect fit for me. I inspired my ring attire from actual Anime characters like Sailor Moon. However with time, I noticed that too many people started to use cosplay as gear. There were even some girls that looked exactly like me. I then changed little dresses and skirts for pants, change hair color and so on. I always modify my character to stay unique."

In 2009 LuFisto added a manager named Pegaboo, a doll she carries to the ring with her. It was unique for the time, but she's already looking ahead. "Today, I see people with dolls too much. Things will have to change again. I believe you must stay one step ahead and that there has to be a constant evolution."

Many wrestlers like LuFisto develop characters who are an extension of their true selves, but some wrestlers go in the opposite direction. Cherry Bomb describes her character as, "That girl you hated in high school who always had her stuff together and was never nice to anyone." Like her favorite WWE Diva Sunny, Cherry puts on a smile and rips the fans for not looking as good as she does. That's a far cry from the girl who wore plaid pants, combat boots, and a pink mohawk at her all girls Catholic high school.

Marc Hauss wrestles under his real name, but initially he adopted the last name Krieger, which means warrior in German. "I had a nickname in college of being 'Every Ladies Dream' and decided to go with it since I was a Rick Rude fan. At the time many guys in the area had pretty generic gear and I really prided myself on sticking out as much as possible. My attire ended up being fully custom airbrushed tights and when I came out for my entrance I wore a tear away white suit and glasses that had my name in rhinestone on them.

"Eventually I went to a Ring of Honor camp, and Brutal Bob Evans asked me why I was not just Marc Hauss. He thought I could really play off it and make it something. I decided to go by my God given name and start wearing trunks which I still wear to this day."

Mickie Knuckles never considered using a fake name in the ring. "My ring name is my real name, given to me at birth. My ring persona has become a mixture of the Mad Hatter, Dr. Jekyll/ Mr. Hyde, and my mother all rolled into one. So basically, it's a personified portion of me."

No one had to invent a personality for Michael Hayes the wrestler; the man and the wrestler are very much one and the same. His charisma and real life story made him a natural babyface and an instant hit with the fans. He wears one legged tights with his prosthetic leg, and he bears the burn scars from an IED on his bare chest. His prosthetic leg gives him the appearance of an underdog, but Hayes has shown he can carry his own with any opponent in the ring. Hayes has a warrior spirit about him, and he's been one of OVW's top stars ever since his debut.

Mitchell Huff bills himself as "The Chosen One," a name inspired by his early days in the business. "Everything I did in the ring came so easy to me, and I usually picked up whatever they were teaching me rather quickly. I always loved the heels growing up and wanted to be one, so I thought of a cocky way to say, 'I was born to do this.'

"My ring attire was inspired by my favorite wrestler, Shawn Michaels. I Googled 'wrestling tights' and found a lady in Tennessee who did Chris Jericho's and a few other WWE guys. She took a lot longer than she said, but when I got the gear it was exactly what I wanted and was very high quality."

Before "The Chosen One" made his debut at D1W in New Albany, promoter Rick Brady decided to pair him with a manager. Managers are often paired with wrestlers who are young, inexperienced, or less skilled on the mic. Brady really wanted to put "The Chosen One" over with the fans, and a solid heel manager was just what he needed.

Enter T.J. Moreschi, a Louisville-based actor with dozens of independent films to his credit. T.J. and Rick Brady had been friends for years, and even though T.J. had no experience in the wrestling world, Rick had always wanted to use him. "I finally agreed to do it on one condition," said T.J. "I wanted to do the bit Earthquake did when he premiered. The British Bulldog and another guy had a pushup contest, and they pulled Earthquake out of the audience to sit on their backs while they did pushups. Earthquake ended up squashing the Bulldog."

Rick invited T.J. to training night, where he asked T.J. to get in the ring and introduce Mitchell. He climbed in the ring and did as asked, completely off the cuff. T.J. loves improvisation and is very comfortable ad-libbing. He and Mitchell made an instant connection, and T.J. has enjoyed every minute of it.

"Right now, my job has me working weekends," he says. "I'm looking for something during the week so I can go out on the road with Mitch."

It takes trial and error to build a successful character. Some changes are thought out and carefully tested, while others come as happy accidents. Hy Zaya is often billed as the "Hood Ninja," a nickname that began in part thanks to an appearance for Juggalo Championship Wrestling.

"I was wrestling Chris Hero in one of those 'Who the f— are these guys?' matches," Hy Zaya says. "The crowd didn't know who we were, and neither did the announcers. They were ripping us to shreds. I was watching the playback when I heard one of the commentators describe me as a Ninja. It felt right. I was like, yeah, that's me. I'm the ninja."

At the end of the day, a wrestler's character is all about getting over. It's about drawing money at the box office and making the fans care. James Harris would never have made the money Kamala did. Yokozuna would never have been the monster heel if he remained Rodney Anoa'i. And imagine if Dwayne Johnson had never become The Rock. You may never see the names Marc Hauss, The Chosen One, or even "Crazy" Mary Dobson on WWE, but the reputation they build with those names may be enough to earn a coveted WWE contract and a new WWE trademarked name to boot.

Ian Rotten takes the plunge against John Wayne Murdoch.
(Photo courtesy Marked Out Photography.)

Cherry Bomb and Kimber Bombs, aka Kimber Lee.
(Photo courtesy Ichiban Drunk.)

The Chosen One and Mr. Mo-licious.
(Photo courtesy Michael Herm Photography.)

Marc Hauss.
(Photo courtesy Marc Hauss.)

Lylah Lodge as May Belle Smothers.
(Photo courtesy Michael Herm Photography.)

DJ Hyde works over Ron Mathis at CZW.
(Photo courtesy Ichiban Drunk.)

"Crazy" Mary Dobson.
(Photo courtesy Ichiban Drunk.)

Colt Cabana on a return visit to IWA Mid-South.
(Photo courtesy Marked Out Photography.)

"The Blackanese Assassin" Menace.
(Photo courtesy Marked Out Photography.)

LuFisto applies the elbow to Nicole Savoy.
(Photo courtesy Ichiban Drunk.)

Tyson Dux with Sin Cara in his clutches.
(Photo courtesy Tyson Dux.)

Eric Emanon puts the grips on his opponent.
(Photo courtesy Eric Emanon.)

Mickie Knuckles shows Hy Zaya who's the boss.
(Photo courtesy Marked Out Photography.)

Mitch Page buries Zodiak in a pile of steel chairs.
(Photo courtesy Marked Out Photography.)

"REMEMBER THAT ONE NIGHT..."

One of the most entertaining matches I ever saw live took place at a TV taping for OVW. The heel tag team of Shiloh Jonze and Raul Espinoza was on the rocks, with both men blaming the other for a recent loss. In a backstage video clip, the two decided to settle their issue in the ring.

Jonze and Espinoza were not just heels, but dirty heels, and both men unloaded all their dirty tricks in a one on one match. First Jonze went for a pin with his feet on the ropes. Then Espinoza did the same. Jonze went for a roll up pulling the tights. Espinoza reversed and pulled Jonze's tights. Time after time, the ref refused to give a three count, insisting the men stop cheating.

One man raced out of the ring, going for a steel chair. As the ref yelled at him to put the chair down, the other man untied the cushion on the turnbuckle. The ref stopped him from exposing the turnbuckle, but by this time, the other man was back in the ring with a chain. A tug of war for the chain ensued. The ref grabbed the chain and turned to throw it away, giving Espinoza the opportunity he needed to hit Jonze in the crotch. The ref never saw it, and Espinoza got the win.

Every fan has a few matches that they never forget, matches they'll share with others for years to come. Wrestlers are the same way. If you stick with it long enough you'll have nights you'll never forget. Some are memorable for how great they are, and some for how completely ridiculous they were.

Chris Hero had a memorable match early on in his career, the kind a young wrestler eager to get noticed takes on without question. "I was wrestling in Indianapolis for a guy named Judas, who billed himself as Kamala, Jr.," remembers Hero. "He came into the locker room and said,

"I'm looking for a guy willing to do a Loser Swallows a Goldfish Match!' I threw my hand up and said, 'I'll do it!'"

Much to Hero's chagrin, Judas went to the pet shop and bought two goldfish. Nevertheless, the young Hero wrestled Filthy the Clown and swallowed two goldfish that night for a measly twenty bucks.

Hero and Colt Cabana shared a very memorable night in Indianapolis with Chuck E. Smooth and CM Punk. The four were offered $150 each, the biggest payday any of the young stars had ever had. The promoter was a fan with money who, like so many, thought he knew how to run a wrestling show. This promoter not only wanted to run a show, but run each of the matches.

"We got to Indy, and we found this college ruled piece of paper written in cursive detailing Chuck E's match," says Chris Hero. "He wanted Chuck E. to botch a shooting star press. Chuck E. had never been to the top ropes in his life. Punk took one look at it, laughed, and threw it in the trash."

By bell time only fourteen people were in the audience, and only four of them had paid. A few of the non-paying viewers were friends of the wrestlers backstage. Those who were there enjoyed a show that they and the wrestlers would never forget.

Chuck E. and Punk were working heel that night and ended up in the ring with Colt, double teaming him. Hero was to run in and make the save, but when he ran down the entry way, he slipped on something spilled on the floor and slid all the way under the ring. Hero took a moment to compose himself before rolling out from under the apron yelling, "Surprise, bitches!"

The match ended up as a Falls Count Anywhere free for all. Hero felt something hit him in the back of the head and instinctively sold the blow, only to realize he had been hit in the back of the head with a cardboard box.

"I had tears in my eyes during that match," recalls Colt Cabana. "I couldn't stop laughing."

As funny as the tag match was, the boys were upstaged by Mad Man Pondo. Pondo paused in the middle of an in-ring promo to go to the restroom. Pondo was on a wireless mic, and yes, he took the mic with him. "They had a guy follow me in the bathroom with a camera," says Pondo. "He asked if I was gonna wash my hands. I told him, 'Why?? I don't care about my opponent!'"

Pondo and his opponent battled out into the parking lot that night. "One of the fans yelled, 'Use my car!' I pointed at the car, asked if it was his. The guy nodded yes, so I suplexed, power bombed, and pile driver my opponent on the car. Turned out later it wasn't the fan's car. It was Drake Younger's dad's car. I got paid and got out of there just as the cops were getting there!"

Ladder matches are one of the most common gimmick matches used in pro wrestling today, but while working for Next Era Wrestling, Eric Emanon took part in a unique variation on the ladder match. "They called it a Banana Tree Match. I was a part of a tag team called Spot Monkeys, Inc., and this was supposed to be our advantage against the other team. They built two massive trees on opposite sides of the ring that were like 15 feet tall from the ring apron. The trees were made out of decently thick PVC piping and painted brown to look like banana trees. The point of the match was to climb the trees and grab a banana or two and get them into your bucket. Team with the most bananas in their bucket when the time expired was the winner. It was ridiculous, but the crowd loved it."

"One of the biggest thrills for me was wrestling Sabu," said Hy Zaya. "Sabu was one of my heroes. I studied his matches a lot, and I stole just about everything he ever did. Our paths crossed many times over the years, but he always had to be reminded who I was. That changed after I finally got in the ring with him."

When Destination One Wrestling booked Hy Zaya against Sabu, he did not take the gift lightly. He watched hours of Sabu's matches, in particular his matches against

African American 2 Cold Scorpio, another of Hy Zaya's heroes. Prior to their match that night, Sabu met with Hy Zaya to ask if he had anything he wanted to do.

"I've stolen just about everything from you," admitted Hy Zaya. Sabu smiled, pleased.

"He gave me a lot of rope," said Hy Zaya. "He really let me work on him. I even busted him open! I kept waiting for him to give me a chair to the face, but he never did."

Sabu is known for staying in character backstage and has, on occasion, delivered a chair shot backstage to people who annoyed him. That night, Sabu made Hy Zaya look and feel like he belonged. After scoring the pin over the younger man, Sabu lifted Hy Zaya to his feet and raised his hand, a humbling and powerful moment for the Hood Ninja.

Jamin Olivencia has had many memorable matches over the years. "One of my favorite comedy matches had me bodyslamming this guy over and over. Every time I bodyslammed him, he got back up, and I did it again. I slammed him eight times in a row. When he got up after the eighth bodyslam, the referee bodyslammed him!"

Olivencia has had phenomenal matches on television, but the match that came to mind when I asked what was his favorite is one that never aired. "I did a dark match with Bo Dallas for WWE in Nashville," he says. "They let me come out as myself, which was awesome, and they gave us eight minutes. Most of my WWE matches have all been squashes, but that night, I really got to show what I could do.

"I know I impressed WWE, but more than that, I came away feeling like I could really compete on that level. I proved that my personality could win over an arena full of people and that I could deliver a great match with WWE talent." Olivencia is grateful to WWE and to Bo Dallas for that opportunity.

"Crazy" Mary Dobson says the best matches so far in her career came with LuFisto. The pair wrestled three times during the summer of 2014, and LuFisto brought out the very best in her each time. "She said she liked me because I reminded her of herself," says Mary. "We both love being dropped on our heads!"

"The wildest match I ever did must have been the Cage of Death," says LuFisto, "Because until the last minute, I didn't even know I was going to be in there. I had a six man tag match early that evening. When I came backstage, John Zandig came to me and said, 'Are you ready for the cage, kid?' I was like, 'What?' John said, 'You will take the mic and include yourself in the Cage of Death with Lobo, Nick Gage, and me.' And that was it. I got inside the massive structure with panes of glass, weapons brought by the fans, light tubes. You name it!"

That brings us to the most infamous of gimmick matches, the deathmatch. Deathmatches are bloody, brutal affairs in which two wrestlers destroy one another with all manner of implements of destruction. I asked Vic Filpot of the Indy Power Rankings to provide me a sampling of the most outrageous deathmatches he has ever witnessed. Here are some of the matches Vic has witnessed with his own eyes.

Barbed Wire Ropes: Barbed wire is wrapped around all the ropes.

No Rope Barbed Wire: All the ropes are replaced with barbed wire.

No Ropes Barbed Wire Salt: The ropes are replaced with barbed wire, and salt is sprinkled around the canvas.

Barbed Wire Bat: A baseball bat wrapped with barbed wire is in the middle of the ring, and the wrestlers race to see who gets to it first to use it.

Barbed Wire Boards: Two boards wrapped in barbed wire are placed in the ring to be used at any time.

Barbed Wire Tables: Tables around ringside are wrapped in barbed wire.

Barbed Wire Canvas: Barbed wire is strung across the canvas.

Barbed Wire Boards and Barbed Wire Bats: Baseball bats and boards are wrapped with barbed wire. Lard may also be spread across the mat to make it slippery.

Barbed Wire Dog Collar Match: Opponents have a dog collar with barbed wire wrapped around the chain to use on one another.

London Bridges: A barbed wire net is placed across the top of the ring.

Thumbtacks: This match may have a pit of thumbtacks In the middle of the ring or tacks sprinkled all over the mat.

Thumbtack Bats and Barbed Wire Boards: Baseball bats with thumbtacks attached and boards with barbed wire wrapped around them are spread throughout the ring.

Barbed Wire Madness: Various objects are wrapped with barbed wire and used in the match. Can also be done as Thumbtack Madness.

Caribbean Spider Net: Barbed wire ropes are used on two sides of the ring. The other two sides are empty but have spider nets: a pit with barbed wire weaved like a spiderweb with broken glass and light tubes beneath.

Pool of Rubbing Alcohol: The ropes are replaced with barbed wires, and kiddie pool of rubbing alcohol is placed in the middle ring.

Electrified Light Bulbs: Barbed wire replaces all the ropes, and strings of electrified lights hang from the wire.

Light Tubes: Dozens of fluorescent light tubes are used as weapons in the match.

Light Tubes Ropes: Fluorescent light tubes lined across the ropes.

Light Tube Tables: Tables with light tubes taped to them are placed around the outside of the ring.

Electrified Light Tube: Electrified light tubes are spread around ringside area.

Light Tubes and Ladders: Self-explanatory, I think.

Light Tubes, Barbed Wire Ropes, Tables, and Scaffolds: Again, self-explanatory.

Lumberjack Light Tube: The ring is surrounded by other wrestlers armed with fluorescent light tubes that they use when someone is tossed out of the ring.

House of Pain: More than 200 light tubes attached to the ropes around the ring, creating four walls of light tubes.

Light Tube Coffin: The winner is the one who can put their opponent into a giant coffin filled with light tubes.

Barefoot: Wrestlers fight barefooted in a mat covered with Legos, thumbtacks, broken glass, etc.

Cinder Block: Stacked cinder blocks are placed in the ring. They are usually set on fire.

Deep Six: Fish hooks are hung from the ropes.

Home Run Derby: A match that can included any number of gimmicks involving baseball bats.

Home Improvement: Tools and home improvement items become weapons in this match.

Unlucky Seven Staple Gun Match: The first person to staple seven dollar bills to his opponent wins.

Balcony Deathmatch: The finishing move has to be done off the balcony.

Cactus: Cacti are spread around the ring.

Bed of Nails: A giant bed of nails is set in the middle of the ring.

Lit Cigarettes and Hot Coals: Pits of lit cigarettes and coals are placed on the outside of the ring.

Flaming Tables: The winner is the first to set a table on fire and put their opponent through it.

Flaming Casket: To win this match, you must put your opponent in a casket and set it on fire.

Death from Above: Different weapons are staged on the top of poles in each turnbuckle.

Taipei Deathmatch: Fists are taped up and dipped in broken glass.

Drunken Deathmatch: The match starts with each wrestler taking five shots of whatever hard drink they choose. Every three to five minutes, they take another shot. This match has been combined with other match types, including scaffolds, Taipei, fans bring the weapons.

Curt Hennig Taipei Deathmatch: A Drunken Taipei deathmatch once held in honor of the late Mr. Perfect. Dean Ambrose was one of the two combatants.

Four Corners of Pain: All four sides of the ring have a pit of dangerous items. Items vary but usually include tacks, barbed wire, light tubes and mousetraps.

Fans Bring the Weapons: Fans create and bring their own weapons to give to the wrestlers.

Toy Box: Wrestlers use kids toys on each other. This can be combined with Fans Bring the Weapons, where the fans bring toys. Legos are usually involved.

Circus Deathmatch: A trampoline made of barbed wire is stretched over the top of the ring ropes, and a tall scaffold is set up over the ring. The loser is the guy who falls from the scaffold onto the trampoline.

Pool of Leaches: A pool with live leaches is set up in the middle of the ring. Variations include Pool of Lobsters and Pool of Piranha.

Not exactly Monday Night Raw material, right?

Zodiak has made a nice career working exactly these types of matches. "I've been in body bag matches, barbwire matches, tacks, no DQ street fights, and dance offs. Some of the most brutal have been strap matches and lumber jack strap matches, including some where the fans get to use the straps. One time a promoter auctioned off straps to fans and let them be the lumber jacks. That was NOT fun. Casket matches are always fun as well. As odd as it sounds, I would like to do a house of horrors match and recently have been discussing doing Flaming Tables. If possible I would love to do one of the first legit buried alive matches on the independent circuit."

Deathmatches still have a strong following. CZW's deathmatch shows are still their top money makers every year. But like any gimmick match, they are best used sparingly, and only by those who know what they are doing.

"The problem with deathmatches today is that the guys doing them see it as an easy way into the business," says Rotten. "These guys are willing to take a fall into sharp objects, but they don't know how to protect each other. One of those young punks broke a Commodore 64 keyboard on the back of my head a few years ago. Everyone knows you don't hit a guy in the back of the head. Pondo, Necro Butcher, and I, we knew how to do it right. We looked out for each other. And we knew how to wrestle."

Mad Man Pondo took two very memorable bumps in deathmatches. During a tag match with IWA Mid-South, he was bodyslammed into a television. The impact of the crash and the shattering glass didn't bother him, but the TV, which was unplugged and had been for weeks, still had an electrical charge stored inside. "Soon as I hit the TV, I could feel the jolt," he says.

The electrical shock distracted him just long enough to mess up his next bump. "I was supposed to catch a bowling ball and pretend it hit my head, but I was late catching it and took a hard knock to the head.

The other happened in CZW, and it is the stuff of legend. "Someone took a wooden board and stuck all these sharpened pencils, sharp points up, on the board," he says. "It sat around for a while, and no one was willing to take a bump with it. Then one night I heard Necro

Butcher say he wasn't going anywhere near it. When I heard Necro say he wasn't going to use it, I knew I had to."

If you search online, you can find the video of Pondo being body slammed on and through the board of sharpened pencils. To this day, he still has graphite in his body, along with huge purple scar right next to his crack. One of Pondo's regular travel buddies shared a very touching anecdote about Pondo's "condition."

"When he and 'Crazy' Mary first got together, he would always back out of the room when he got out of bed. He didn't want her to see the scar and think he had a turd stuck to his butt."

HEROES AND LEGENDS

To this point we've mainly discussed the young stars of professional wrestling, the men and women eager to make a name for themselves and rise to the top of the card. Promoters know that while the younger wrestlers are the ones who can truly give you a show, they are rarely enough to draw a crowd, especially from fans of TV wrestling. Attracting those fans means booking a "name," and there are plenty of names to choose from on the independent circuit.

Every time WWE cuts a wrestler, they create an instant draw for a smaller independent. Guys like John Morrison, Evan Bourne, and Brodus Clay wait out their no-compete clauses and make their way to the independent scene where they get much greater star treatment than they did at the top. What's more, many old school stars are still around to main event and give the rub to younger talent: Southern stars like Bobby Fulton, Tracy Smothers, and Ricky Morton; ECW stars like Jerry Lynn, Sabu, and Tommy Dreamer; and even WWF stars like Tito Santana, Nikolai Volkoff, and Sunny.

Working with a legend is a treat for the wrestlers as well as the fans – usually. With every new encounter there's a chance you're going to have your childhood idol smashed to pieces. "Any time you meet one of those guys," says Ian Rotten, "you just hope they're not gonna be an a—hole." Fortunately, most of the older stars are not only good people, but great mentors to the new generation. They know the kids across from them in the ring are the future of the business, and they're very supportive.

"I've had the ability to work shows with people like Tommy Dreamer, Danny Doring, Shane Douglas, Scotty 2 Hotty, Al Snow, Jerry Lynn and quite a few others," says

Eric Emanon. "They have been nothing but helpful and are more than happy to share their knowledge and experiences in their careers with you."

"My first match with a vet was The Boogie Woogie Man, Jimmy Valiant," says Menace. "He was fun and very easy to work with. I learned that night how to not do a lot, tell a story, and please a crowd. I've had the pleasure of working with Dr. Tom Pritchard, Tracy Smothers, Vic the Bruiser, Jimmy Golden, Kid Kash, Jerry Lynn, Christopher Daniels, Rob Conway, and Shane Douglas just to name a few. I also teamed up with Ricky Morton. All those guys I learned something new from, and was honored to be in the ring with them."

Marc Hauss had the privilege of working with Brutus "The Barber" Beefcake and Hurricane Helms. He even got a haircut from the Barber following his match. "Beefcake was easy. It was awesome to have the haircut and be a part of something I watched on tapes as a child. Hurricane was my favorite. I was able to pick his brain all day alone and then work with him in a quality match. We stayed in contact, and I've been able to ask him questions. He takes the time to respond and helps me out. That means a lot."

DJ Hyde has worked with many veterans, and he has several he leans on as a wrestler and a promoter. "Any time I need to talk, I can call Al Snow, Tommy Dreamer, and even Paul Heyman. They've been great to me."

Ian Rotten was in his early twenties when he booked one of his great heroes for IWA Mid-South, Dusty Rhodes. Rhodes proved to be a gracious guest, who called Ian a week later to thank him for the booking and the beer in his hotel fridge. But it was when they were planning their tag match that Rhodes made the deepest impression on the young promoter. "He said, 'How about when it's time for the finish, I throw you the elbow pad, and you do the Atomic Elbow?' When he said that, it was like I could hear angels singing from Heaven!"

Rotten had equal praise for another WWE Hall of Famer, the late Eddie Guerrero. "Eddie came to us after a very public firing with the WWE, but despite having been at the top, he was a very humble guy. One night I had to ask him if he'd give me a break on his price so I could pay the other guys on the card. He told me to give him what I had. When I gave him the money, he counted out half and gave it back to me for the boys."

Eddie's last match in IWA Mid-South was a three way with Colt Cabana and CM Punk. "He knew he was going back to WWE the next day, and he knew they were putting the Intercontinental title on him. He told me he was going to go easy in the ring, and I was fine with that, but when he got in there, he was flying around the same as the other guys. I asked him why he changed his mind, and he told me, 'I couldn't let those kids show me up!'"

Rotten is now in his twentieth year as a promoter. He's made his share of enemies, but he's also been a hero and mentor to many young stars, including CM Punk, Colt Cabana, Chris Hero, and more recently Reed Bentley. When Rotten had to have a toe amputated in the summer of 2014, it was Bentley who stepped up to help shuttle Ian to all his follow-ups and doctor's appointments. "He's my best friend, and my brother," says Bentley. "He's done so much for me, booking me with Chris Hero, Kevin Sullivan, Jeff Jarrett, Ricky Morton. I owe him a lot."

Hy Zaya had a very humbling encounter with Rotten early in his career. When he got his first break with IWA Mid-South, Hy Zaya was the youngest guy in the locker room. He came in with an attitude, an unbroken spirit that came from his days working in backyards. "I had a lot of wrong ideas about the business," he admits. "I thought you got to decide for yourself what you'd do and wouldn't do, whom you'd wrestle and what would happen."

Hy Zaya walked out of the locker room one night, very displeased with his booking. Before he could reach his car, Corporal Robinson chased him down. "You better get back in there before Ian knows you're gone!" Robinson shouted.

Hy Zaya followed his mentor back inside, but it was too late. Ian rained profanities down on the young upstart, reminding him of his place in the pecking order. "You may be good at that backyard wrestling crap, but when it comes to real wrestling, you're nothing!!"

Corporal Robinson did more than just save Hy Zaya's career that night. He is one of many veterans Hy Zaya credits with teaching him the business and teaching him how to survive it. "I've been offered all kinds of drugs. Steroids, cocaine. A girl tried to blow some powder in my face one night. "Those guys looked out for me: Necro Butcher, Harry Palmer, Mad Man Pondo, American Kickboxer, Mitch Page, Bull Pain. They kept me out of trouble."

Tracy Smothers is a former Memphis star who works countless indie shows a year. Smothers works very hard not only to entertain the fans, but to encourage the young stars he works with. "It's funny because when I watched Tracy on TV, I hated him," says Hy Zaya. "He was that Southern guy with the Confederate flag, always shooting his mouth off. But Tracy's been one of my go-to guys for advice and support."

Hy Zaya's not the only one with high praise for Tracy Smothers. Promoters and wrestlers share stories of how much Smothers cares for the future of the business. Smothers takes a keen interest in the young guys in the locker room, often sitting in the gorilla position right behind the curtain so he can watch every match. He's eager to see the young stars grow, and he's not shy about handing out praise.

Smothers works very hard in the ring to put the young talent over as well. When the fans chant, "Tracy sucks," Tracy turns the negative chant around so the fans are cheering the babyface. "I don't care if y'all chant, 'Tracy sucks,' just don't chant, 'Go Hy Zaya go!'"

"Tracy put me over in a match," says Austin Bradley. "It was such great match where I didn't have to think. I just listened and followed his lead."

Another veteran cited by many young stars for his influence is Mad Man Pondo. After Austin Bradley left OVW, he became very discouraged and was close to quitting. Then he met Pondo.

"I was booked to work a tag match with Pondo," he says. "I was scared to death of him. I knew him by his reputation, all those deathmatches. This was a man who had once fallen in a pit of barbed wire.

Pondo was impressed with Bradley. After the show, he offered to take Austin to another show. Pondo continued to bring Bradley along on bookings and even got him in with Juggalo Championship Wrestling. "He's been a great encourager to me."

"I've never seen myself as a mentor," Pondo says when asked about his influence on the next generation. "I was a gimmick guy for a long time. Now I have guys coming up to me asking what I would do in this situation and that. I think they see 'Crazy' Mary's success and think that I'm somehow responsible for it. But that's all her."

"Crazy" Mary disagrees. "He's too nice. He really is the nicest guy. He did a match recently with three younger guys, two age 21 and one 19. He could have squashed them if he wanted. Instead, he's the one out there selling them, taking all these crazy bumps."

Not every veteran is friendly, and not every young star is open to the feedback and wisdom the veterans can offer. Still, the majority of younger wrestlers look to the veterans for advice, and the veterans are more than willing to not only advise, but put their successors over. "That's what veterans are supposed to do," says Mickie Knuckles. "Teach what they have learned to the next generation."

One of Hy Zaya's most inspirational encounters was with Jerry Lynn. Lynn never became a huge household name despite having a championship run in the

WWE, but the ECW legend is one of the most respected workers and mentors on the independent circuit. Prior to a training class led by Lynn, who was retired at the time, Hy Zaya asked if Lynn had any regrets about walking away. Lynn told Hy Zaya, "I feel bad, because I feel like there's still so much I could learn."

Lynn's sentiments made a deep impression on Hy Zaya. "If Jerry Lynn, who has been everywhere and wrestled everyone, says he has a lot to learn, how much more do I have to learn?"

The wrestlers of today owe a lot to those who have gone before. Most are eager to learn from the veterans they work with, and all of them get a thrill when they meet their heroes.

"One of the biggest thrills of my career was when I met Sabu," says "Crazy" Mary. "I went to shake his hand, and he looked at me and said, '"Crazy" Mary, right?' I couldn't believe he knew my name!"

ON THE ROAD

Wrestlers spend very little time in the ring. Except in rare circumstances, wrestlers usually only work five to fifteen minutes in the ring, depending on where they are on the card. During the week, they put in a few hours here and there training, either in the gym or the ring, but the overall amount of time spent doing something athletic is very minimal.

So where do wrestlers spend most of their time? Driving. You can't become a full-time wrestler living and working in one town. You have to be on the road, traveling anywhere and everywhere you can get booked.

Not surprisingly, wrestlers have some great stories about life on the road. It's on these long road trips that bonds are formed and ribs are pulled. It's here that wrestlers make some of their favorite memories.

Aaron Williams spent a lot of time on the road with Sami Callihan and Jon Moxley before they were signed by WWE. "Moxley's one of my best friends. He was there for me when I went through a really rough time."

That's not to say Moxley's the opposite of his WWE persona, Dean Ambrose. "The Lunatic Fringe" had a ritual he followed whenever it was his turn to drive. "We'd fill up at Speedway, where we both collected Speedway points. He would buy a cappuccino, a Mountain Dew, and a banana. He sat in the driver's seat, put the coffee between his legs, the Mountain Dew in a cup holder, peeled the banana, and pulled out his phone. Then he would drive 90 down the highway while eating, drinking, and talking on the phone. Somehow, I never worried about it, and we always got there safely."

Austin Bradley remembers a bonding experience he had with a tag team partner on one of their first road trips together. "I was still pretty green in the business when I got paired up with Kyle Maverick. We rode together to a show in Goshen, Indiana. We barely knew each other. As were rolling down the highway, 'Separate Ways' by Journey came on. Kyle turned it up and started playing air piano. Next thing you know, we're both rocking out to Journey. It was our bonding moment, and Kyle became my first real brother in the wrestling business."

Picking the right travel partner is important if you want to arrive safe and sane. "The first time I took my youngest daughter on the road," says Apollo Garvin, "We rode with my tag team partner JB Thunder and another guy, Cliff Hanger. We had a four hour drive to Tennessee, and Cliff didn't shut up the entire ride. He talked from the moment we picked him up until the moment we arrived. Even my daughter noticed and asked me, "Does this guy ever shut up?"

Any hope of a quiet ride home quickly vanished when they got in the car after the show. "He started talking again and talked the whole way home. Finally, about fifteen minutes from his house, he announced that he was tired and was going to shut his eyes for a bit. He closed his eyes, and we all breathed a sigh, thankful for the break. Fifteen seconds later, his eyes opened. So did his mouth. He talked the rest of the way home."

Austin Bradley had no problem with the six guys he rode with on one trip, nor did his friends normally have a problem with him. There were six guys piled into a Jeep, including Austin's friend Danno and Kyle Maverick.

Not wanting to be crowded, Austin decided to roll out his sleeping bag in the back cargo area and get some rest. Rest was put aside when Austin discovered a Sharpie and a writing tablet. He wrote the words "HELP ME" in big letters on the tablet and began flashing the sign to other drivers as they passed by. Austin would scream and yell to get the other drivers' attention as well, all the time keeping his sign hidden from the others.

Before long, the Jeep was surrounded by a car and a couple of large trucks, all with angry drivers screaming for Danno to pull over. When the others discovered why and how Austin was responsible, they were furious. As Danno frantically tried to weave through the vehicles pinning them in and make an escape, Maverick shouted back to Austin, "If we get pulled over by the cops, you better be bleeding!!"

One of the most dangerous things you can do while traveling is fall asleep. You become fair game for a car full of wrestlers looking to entertain themselves. "Recently we were driving home from Pennsylvania, about a five hour drive for us," says Eric Emanon. "I was at the wheel, and I warned everyone, 'If you fall asleep, we are going to mess with you.' With about an hour left in the drive, my buddy Xavier Fate fell asleep. I told the other guys quietly that on the count of three we were going to scream at the top of our lungs and I was going to spike the brakes. I counted down and executed the plan to perfection. I've never heard a man shriek in terror so loud in my entire life. He said that he had 'Mommy braced' himself across the dudes in the back by throwing his arms out and bracing for impact. He then called me an a—hole and was wide awake the rest of the trip. We laughed about it for the next half hour."

"My most memorable road trip had to be my first trip to Tennessee," says Mitchell Huff. "I was traveling with Tank Toland, Rich Young, and Romeo Roselli. I drove the three hour trip, and Tank gave us all kinds of stories about his time in the WWE, his time in 'wrestlers court,' and all kinds of cool behind the scenes stuff. It was like a three hour uncut raw shoot interview. I was in Heaven.

"After the show, the four of us went to out to eat and had fun with the waitress. We had her convinced that we were strippers. We all had special talents, and each special talent was really bizarre. My special talent involved being able to do something incredibly sexy with some mini blinds. The waitress was begging to see it. Of course I had nothing to show her, but Romeo called me "Blinds" the duration of the trip."

One of LuFisto's favorite road memories happened during an overnight stay. "There was a midget wrestler on a tour that was so drunk. He was laying butt naked up in the air on the floor. We threw him out of the room. He started running and hitting every door in the hallway screaming, 'Let me in!' He then fell asleep on the floor in the hall, still naked!"

"For some reason I always find it fun and an adventure to stay in the worst possible motels," says Zodiak. It makes it interesting, and if you're on a slim budget, you may as well make it fun and exciting. I can remember staying in hotels that ran $25 a night and having to put chairs against the doors to make sure it was 'safe.' It's that or sleep in the car. I've done that many times."

Hy Zaya took a little ribbing on his first real road trip. The rookie rode in the back of a U-Haul with Harry Palmer and the man he considers his sensei, American Kickboxer. "We were hauling the ring to Missouri. My first time. And the guys started telling me about the One Armed Shooter."

The One Armed Shooter was a dangerous female fan, a one armed woman who didn't like rookies and despised bad wrestling. If she didn't like a wrestler's performance, she would attack the weak performer with her one good arm and beat him savagely.

The vets also warned Hy Zaya that he would be walking into a very hostile, very racist crowd. Hy Zaya wasn't sure if he should be more frightened by the racist mob or the demonic one armed fan!

Hy Zaya was certain he would be the heel that night. If the crowd truly was racist, nothing he could do would make him a babyface. To his surprise, the crowd popped huge when his entrance music hit. American Kickboxer talked him through the match, and the crowd gave all the competitors a huge ovation at the end.

"I remember walking in the back, getting handshakes from all the guys. It was the first time I really felt a part, like I belonged."

The road is a gauntlet unto itself. It is the place where legends are born, both in the ring and out. One of those legends will unfold for you in the next chapter, a road story so epic, it had to have its own chapter.

Jerrod Harris, innocent victim.
(Photo courtesy Michael Herm Photography.)

A NIGHT IN TENNESSEE WITH PONDO

Early on in the research process, Austin WGS Bradley became one of the first wrestlers to grant me an interview. On the night I did my final in person interviews with Apollo Garvin and T.J. Moreschi, I ran into Austin again. Austin gave me a travel story so epic, I knew it deserved its own chapter.

Several weeks later I was fortunate enough to meet Jerrod Harris, one of the other parties involved in this story. Jerrod shared his side with me, allowing me to tell this tale in even greater depth. Without further ado, here's the story of one night in Tennessee with Mad Man Pondo.

Austin WGS Bradley

Anytime I've been on the road with Mad Man Pondo, our car has broken down. Doesn't matter where we go, or how far, or who's driving, or what car we have. That's not true when "Crazy" Mary is with us. If Mary is with us, we could drive to the coast and back without a hitch. If it's just Pondo, we're going to break down.

One day, Pondo called and asked if I want to go to Tennessee. He was offered $600 to do a show, so my buddy Danno and I decided to go with him.

We drove to the venue in Tennessee, a place that looked like an oil and lube garage. The stage was a piece of crap, and the curtains from the locker room were actual shower curtains.

We went backstage and met the boys we'd be working with. I was matched with a guy named Cannonball, who was about five feet tall and solid as a rock. The two of us talked through our match, but when we got out to the ring, Cannonball forgot everything, including the finish. Cannonball was supposed to go over, so I picked him up for a slam, fell back with him on top of me, and he got the pin.

Backstage again, Cannonball spoke with Pondo. Later on that night, Cannonball was to be part of a group that stormed the ring and attacked Pondo. Cannonball wanted to use a fireball, a small pyrotechnic thrown at the face.

"Have you ever done a fireball?" asked Pondo. Cannonball said no. Pondo shook his head and told Cannonball it wasn't going to happen, but Cannonball insisted. Pondo finally confiscated the fireball, saying, "I'll just hang on to this, okay?"

Pondo finished the show unscathed and unburned, and he collected his money. We hopped in Danno's car for the long ride home. I settled in, ready to get some sleep. That's when the car began to shake.

Danno pulled over and sure enough, we had a flat tire. Danno had a spare in the back, but unfortunately, Danno had just had custom rims installed on his car. The rims were locked with a key, and Danno had left the key at home.

Like I said, any time I've been on the road with Mad Man Pondo, the car breaks down!

We all had our phones on us, but they had all long since run out of batteries.

None of us had a car charger. We were stranded on a dark road in the middle of nowhere. At Pondo's insistence, we started walking. We walked five miles before we finally found anything, a 24 hour Walmart.

We were able to use a phone to call AAA, who sent a tow truck out to find the car. We turned around and walked five miles back to the car.

The truck arrived soon after we got there, but the driver was unable to help us. Without the key, there was no way to get the rims off the car! The tow truck driver left us in the middle of nowhere, no better off than we were before.

A few minutes later, the driver was back. He offered to shuttle the three of us to Walmart if we paid him twenty dollars each. Pondo in the guy's truck with his things, including his signature Stop sign and saw-bat: a baseball bat with a spinning saw blade at the end.

A short while later we were all reunited at Walmart. I got a charger and started charging my phone while Pondo went inside looking for luggage. Pondo had a trip coming up, and he needed something new to carry his saw-bat. Pondo was using the saw-bat to size up different pieces of luggage when a brave Walmart employee approached him.

"Sir," he said, "You can't have that in here."

"What?" said Pondo. "It's just a saw-bat!"

"I'm sorry," said the kid. "You have to take it outside."

Pondo took his saw-bat outside. Around this time our tow truck driver came back and offered to tow the car to Walmart for another twenty. We paid the man while Pondo took the blade off the saw-bat and went back inside to look for luggage. The same kid came over and told him to take the bat outside. "I took the blade off!" said Pondo, but the kid stood his ground.

Danno and I, meanwhile, had gotten our hands on two of the Amigo carts. We found some foam swords and were jousting in the aisles until the store staff told us to clear out.

We all gathered together on a bench outside. Then the tornado sirens went off, and we headed back inside the store.

Finally in the early hours of the morning, we were able to reach our friend Jerrod Harris, a fellow wrestler who was living in Louisville at the time. We explained the situation and told him we needed a lift. We had a show that evening in Illinois, and we had to get home. Jerrod was livid we drug him into this. "I'm going to drive down there and kill you all."

"Well that puts a damper on this night! Pondo railed. "You're gonna drive down here just to kill us? I'm pretty sure I saw Jeepers Creepers right up the road from here. He could do that much for us!"

Jerrod Harris

I was just chilling at my place playing video games when the guys called begging me to drive down and pick them up. They told me they were just a little ways south of

Elizabethtown, which is only a forty-five minute drive from Louisville, but when I got in the car and started messing with my GPS, I discovered they were NOT just south of E-town. They were three and a half hours away!

It's the middle of the night and I'm driving I-65 South. Once you get past E-town, there's very little light on I-65 South. I'm driving in pitch darkness, following my GPS, and I'm very sure I'm going to be murdered.

Austin

As we waited for Jerrod to arrive, Pondo and Danno went off on their own, looking for deathmatch weapons. Danno came up with the idea of sticking a cheese grater on the end of a Wiffleball bat. At this point the store staff had decided best just to give us space, so no one was thrown out into the night.

Jerrod

The guys told me they were in some Wal-Mart in this tiny little town. I went to the first Wal-Mart I saw and went inside. I walked all over that store, peering down every aisle, looking for these guys, and I couldn't find them anywhere. Finally, I walked back outside and saw Danno's vehicle on the other side of the parking lot, as far as he could possibly be from where I parked.

Everyone got in my car and we started back home. There was a lot of traffic on I-65 North at the time, and we were going nowhere fast. My car had no air, and I was burning up inside the car. I started fumbling around on my GPS, looking for any alternate route I could find, just to get some air blowing on my face.

We were getting hungry, and I needed gas, so around 6 AM I stopped at a tiny redneck gas station. Danno gave me twenty bucks for gas. Austin gave me five. Pondo gave me nothing! I spent ten bucks at the McDonalds inside the gas station and used the rest for gas.

Austin

A really hot girl came in the store the same time we did, and Jerrod took an interest in her. He was putting on the charm and using all his best lines like, "Do you like Star Wars?"

Then came Pondo. He walked in the store and saw Jerrod talking to the girl. "Aww, hell, Jerrod went and fell in love!" Pondo went on and on, railing at Jerrod and doing his best to warn the girl off. "Better be careful with him, sweetie. This one works fast. Watch out, or he'll slip a ring on your finger when you're not looking!"

After using the restroom, Pondo came out, grabbed Jerrod and drug him back to the car. Our driver was even more annoyed than before, but thankfully the evening's worst was finally behind us. We rode the rest of the way home in peace, except for Pondo occasionally repeating a phrase he found scrawled on the bathroom stall beneath a Confederate flag. Best to leave that part to your imagination.

Jerrod

We got back to Louisville, and I dropped each guy at their place. As soon as I walked in the door of my place, I collapsed on the couch and went to sleep. I remember telling all three of them that I didn't want to see any of them for a while. Matter of fact, I'm pretty sure I told them I didn't want to see them or any of their family members for at least six days.

If you're like me, you're wondering, what happened to the fireball? Sadly, it seems the fireball never made an appearance the rest of the night. It's probably for the best. A little fireball at the wrong time, and the entire evening could have ended up behind bars, something that never, ever happens to wrestlers on road trips!

LuFisto looking innocent with a steel chair in hand.
(Photo courtesy Ichiban Drunk.)

OVERSEAS

The roots of modern day professional wrestling can be traced all the way back to the Civil War. Wrestling became a popular extracurricular activity in the Union camps, and by the end of the war, a soldier from New York named William Muldoon established himself as the Union champion. After the war Muldoon traveled to Germany, where he enlisted in the German army, where wrestling was also a popular leisure activity. Muldoon learned the European style of wrestling from his brothers in arms before returning to the States to become America's first full-time athlete and professional wrestling champion.

Professional wrestling (or in the corporate vernacular, "sports entertainment") as we now know it originated in the United States, but it has been an international sport from the very beginning. Wrestling itself is one of the oldest sports in the world, and as professional wrestling grew in popularity, every country made the sport in its own image.

Travel overseas offers wrestlers the opportunity to learn new styles and techniques while growing their network of contacts. It gives them a chance to make more money than they could on small bookings here in the States. And yes, it also gives them a chance to see the world.

Chris Hero was in the business a little more than a year when he received his first offer to travel overseas. "I did some TV tapings for Jim Miller in Pittsburgh in my first year as a wrestler," says Chris Hero. "The tapes were sent all over the place. One day I got an email from a guy in Germany, telling me he was going to do the German commentary on these tapes. I wrote him back, and like I always did, I asked if he could pass my name along to anyone he knew who might want to book me."

That email paid dividends, as the rookie soon received an invitation to travel to Germany. He received his plane ticket via email and suddenly realized he needed to get a passport. The promoter had Chris flying out of O'Hare in Chicago, five hours from Chris's then home of Dayton, Ohio. He had his passport photo taken as quickly as he could, but he was told it would not arrive in time for his flight.

"Instead of sending the passport to my home, they sent it to O'Hare in my name," says Hero, who breathed a great sigh of relief when the passport was waiting for him at the airport.

Hero has traveled the world since that first trip to Germany including England, Austria, the Netherlands, Australia, and Japan. To him the best part of travel is making connections with other wrestlers. On his second trip to Germany he met a young Swiss wrestler named Claudio Castagnoli. Hero became a mentor to Claudio, as he does to many young stars, and he became a great encourager to the man known to WWE fans as Cesaro.

The majority of overseas bookings happen through personal connections, but the Internet made getting booked much easier. When Colt Cabana and CM Punk got their first international booking, the promoter who contacted them had never seen them wrestle. His fans discovered the two Chicago natives through YouTube and begged the promoter to book them.

Jamin Olivencia is another wrestler who had the chance to travel early in his career. After about a year with Empire State Wrestling, Jamin was invited to wrestle in England. Olivencia learned a lot from the British grapplers, but it was an incident that took place his first night that left the biggest impression.

"Prior to my match, a few of the guys brought me a glass of orange juice. They said it was a tradition, when a 'Yank' came to England for the first time, to drink a glass of orange juice before their first match. I thanked them for the glass and I drank it.

"Just before I went out for the match, I suddenly had a massive erection! It came out of nowhere, and it just wouldn't go away. I didn't want to walk down to the ring with this huge hard-on, so I grabbed an American flag and covered myself. My opponent kept asking if I was okay. He also kept finding ways to drop me on my belly over, and over, and over.

"Soon as I got to the back, I knew I had been had. 'Was it a hard match, Jamin?' they said. 'You looked a little stiff out there.' Turns out they put eighty milligrams of Viagra in that orange juice!"

While working with Next Era Wrestling, Eric Emanon was invited to travel to Canada and work for Smith Hart of the legendary Hart family. "I wasn't booked to wrestle, but Smith liked my hustle. He asked if I had my gear with me. Any worker knows if he shows up to a show he isn't booked at to always have his gear with him. I worked in the main event against Sniper Randy Vaughn for the World Heavyweight Championship. When I came out to the ring, I was flabbergasted at the crowd they drew. It was at a resort and literally was standing room only from the back end of the indoor restaurant that had these giant garage doors opening to the outside all the way to the ringside security railings. Plus people were pulling up behind the fences and parking golf carts and sitting on top of them to see the action. It was an experience I will never forget."

Cherry Bomb's first international experience required her to travel the opposite way, from her home country of Canada to the United States. Customs is often a challenge for wrestlers, especially those who carry merchandise to sell, and Cherry was always nervous when crossing the border. "When they asked me why I was coming to the US, I said it was to shop. They never questioned it, even when they pulled my wrestling pads out during their inspection."

Many wrestlers tell customs they are just on vacation or visiting friends, hoping they can get through with as little hassle as possible. On one European trip, Adam Cole and three other wrestlers went through customs as a group, saying they were visiting friends and then going on to Germany for Oktoberfest. Customs officials became suspicious of the four young males when they discovered they did not have return flights booked, a major red flag in the post 911 era.

The customs official asked the boys to wait on a bench. Five minutes later, the customs official came storming over to them with paperwork in hand.

"What's your connection to the Filipino government?" the man asked.

The boys were stunned and told the man they did not even know anyone from the Philippines. "Okay," said the man. "What are your hobbies?"

The boys gave some generic answers, hoping to end the interrogation quickly. "We like to work out, we like to party, we like to watch movies."

"Okay, okay," said the man. "So you're not wrestling on the Fight Club Pro Show tonight in Wolverhampton, are you?" To the boys' surprise, the man produced a flier for the show with their names and faces on it.

The boys were let through but not before being taken to another room where they were fingerprinted by a very unprofessional customs agent. "As he was fingerprinting me," says Cole, "He starts telling me who is going to get busted. 'Yeah, you see that guy in the pink jacket? He made a fake visa. Here, look at it!'"

Marc Hauss had a scary encounter of his own while crossing the border US/Canadian border. "There were three of us booked in Detroit at a promotion called AWWL. We were traveling with a wrestler who will remain unnamed who, the day before, had a minor heart attack. He didn't require surgery, but the doctors injected a dye into his body to make sure there was no blockage. He told us about the heart attack but said nothing about the dye. When we hit the border to cross, only a few years after 9/11, we lit up like a Christmas tree in terms of being radioactive. He was pulled out of the car and had to walk through the car scanner separate of us to confirm the story of the heart attack and dye.

"By coincidence, this was also the weekend Canada decided to upgrade the software used for noting cars that crossed the border. The person who had the heart attack also had issues with the border. There were many notes in the computer that explained his situation, but wouldn't you know it, all of those were wiped out that weekend. We crossed the border four times, and every time, we got pulled in and questioned.

"If that wasn't bad enough, we worked four TV tapings that weekend only to find out that there was no pay. It wasn't funny then, but we laugh about it now."

The major international promotions are very hospitable to guests from other countries. Wrestlers are greeted at the airport and shuttled to their lodging. They're housed with other wrestlers from the same country, and they are provided with a translator. Transportation is usually provided as well, but the long rides by bus, car, train, and even ferry can be as tedious as they are in the states.

American wrestlers find eating a challenge in Great Britain. The British do not have as many restaurants, and the food available is nothing like what the Americans are used to. British gyms are also very substandard compared to the gyms available in America. The same is true in Japan, but the major Japanese promoters always provide workout equipment at the shows.

The food is also a highlight for visitors to Japan, according to Tyson Dux. "We would go out to eat at night with sponsors, and the first dish was usually something weird. I've eaten every part of the pig as well as raw horse. I think they did it just to see our reactions."

Marc Hauss had a different food experience in Germany. "When I was in Germany," says Hauss, "They they had a nice fresh spread in the locker room of food made of homemade sandwiches with fresh cold cuts and fruit. Also, they do not drink the tap water there like we do. They drink seltzer water. That was quite a shock coming to the back after my match looking for water. I was halfway through the bottle before I realized it was carbonated."

Mexico made a very different impression on Hauss when he saw how differently the people lived. "Sometimes here in the United States, we complain about not having the newest game system or clothes or having to buy used. In Mexico a lot of people are struggling to get by and just have the necessities. Both experiences, Germany and Mexico, taught me to appreciate what we really have here. They also taught me patience and faith in humanity. I had to try and communicate with many people who did not speak any English and blindly trust people from a different country to take care of me when the only common bond we had was wrestling."

Wrestling matches are also different from country to country. In Great Britain, for example, the rings are smaller, usually fourteen square feet versus twenty feet in America. The British still wrestle in rounds similar to a boxing match. It's an adjustment for American-style wrestlers, but it is by no means a limitation on creative booking.

"In between rounds, the referee would go to the scoring table," recalls Leon White, who wrestled around the world as the monster Big Van Vader. "When he did, I'd run over and hit the babyface from behind. The crowd would go nuts and try to let the ref know what I did. Later on, the babyface would return the favor and get me. The ref would catch him and fine him a thousand marks. Inevitably, one of those German fans would offer to pay the fine. Then at the end of the night, the babyface and I had an extra thousand marks to split!"

"Crazy" Mary Dobson has been all over the world in her brief career. One of her most memorable stops was in Scotland, where she was invited to stay at the home of the promoter and his wife. When she walked in the house, she noticed the front room was full of what looked like a frightening assortment of torture devices. The promoter then introduced Mary to his wife, a professional dominatrix.

"She looked like Elvira," says Mary, "But she was very sweet to me. She made me breakfast my first morning. As we were eating, she told me she had a client coming over. She asked if I wanted to assist. I declined."

When the client arrived, Mary was upstairs watching television with the promoter. "It was very surreal. We were both sitting there, watching *Cops*, while a grown man was screaming in pain downstairs."

Mad Man Pondo's favorite overseas memory happened half the world away in Japan. After the evening's show, he went out to a club with one of the greatest independent stars of all time, Abdullah the Butcher. "Abby had brought along his T-shirts," says Pondo. "He was selling them to the Yakuzas in the club, who were giving them to the dancers."

At about five in the morning, the pair finally decided to head to their hotel. "Abby looked up and saw the hotel, so he suggested we walk. That was unusual for Abdullah, but the streets of Tokyo at 5 AM are safer than most streets in America.

"We were walking down the sidewalk, and I was carrying his T-shirt box. We spotted another man walking toward us smoking a cigarette. The man got close enough to see us and he stopped and pointed at Abdullah.

"'Abdullah?' he said. Abby said yes. 'Abdullah the Butcher?' Abby said yes. All of the sudden, the man starts screaming, 'Abdullah the Butcher! Abdullah the Butcher!'

"Suddenly, all the dark buildings on the street began to light up. People were waking up, turning on their lights, and looking outside. Soon they were flooding into the streets, all eager to get a glimpse of Abdullah the Butcher.

Abby turned to me and said, 'Pondo! Give me a T-shirt!' Next thing I knew, we were selling Abdullah's T-shirts in the streets of Tokyo at 5 AM in the morning."

It's never easy to venture out of your comfort zone, but every wrestler who travels overseas comes away richer for the experience. It's a learning experience inside and outside of the ring, making them not only better wrestlers, but an ideal source of knowledge for anyone who might travel abroad.

"I learned that when all else fails, a nice snug shot will always win the fans over," says Mickie Knuckles. "And never ride on the Autoban when you're high and drunk. SCARY!"

Eric Emanon prepares to fly.
(Photo courtesy Eric Emanon.)

Aaron Williams.
(Photo courtesy Ichiban Drunk.)

Adam Cole.
(Photo courtesy Ichiban Drunk.)

Mickie Knuckles takes out the trash.
(Photo courtesy Marked Out Photography.)

Tyson Dux.
(Photo courtesy Tyson Dux.)

Zodiak.
(Photo courtesy Marked Out Photography.)

Mad Man Pondo and Tracy Smothers.
(Photo courtesy Michael Herm Photography.)

Lylah Lodge and cupcakes at the gimmick table.
(Photo courtesy Lylah Lodge.)

Reed Bentley takes a boot from Hy Zaya.
(Photo courtesy Marked Out Photography.)

Mitch Johnson and Austin WGS Bradley.
(Photo courtesy Michael Herm Photography.)

Yes, those are MegaBloks waiting for Christian Skyfire to land at the 2014 King of the Deathmatch Tournament.
(Photo courtesy Marked Out Photography.)

LuFisto vs. Jordynne Grace at the 2014 Queen of the Deathmatch Tournament.
(Photo courtesy Marked Out Photography.)

Marc Hauss on his way to the ring.
(Photo courtesy Ubel Photography.)

Melvin Maximus and Jamin Olivencia backstage at OVW. (Photo courtesy Jamin Olivencia.)

THE FANS

One time in Memphis, Jerry Lawler came up with the idea to do a fight with Terry Funk in the empty Mid-South Coliseum. The two men met with just a camera man and fought all over the building. It was original, but it turned out to be much more difficult than Lawler or Funk realized. They had total freedom to go where they wanted to do what they wanted, but in the end, the match just felt flat to them.

The match wasn't missing a storyline, or even high spots. It was missing the energy that only comes from a live crowd.

Fans are a vital component to professional wrestling, and not just because they're the ones who buy the tickets. Wrestling is a spectator sport. Wrestlers feed off the cheers and boos of the crowd. Fans can make or break a match, a wrestler, even a whole promotion with their wallets and their energy.

Ironically, there are some places where the wrestling fans are the most dangerous part of the match. The old ECW crowd was known for being very vocal and raucous, and in the old territory days Memphis and Mid-South Wrestling could be very dangerous. If a crowd didn't like what they saw, they'd pelt the ring with garbage or worse, storm the ring. It was so bad in Louisville during the 1970s police wore riot gear to escort the heels to and from the ring!

All of that seems like child's play to those who work for Juggalo Championship Wrestling. Founded and owned by the Insane Clown Posse, JCW has a well-deserved reputation as one of the most violent and aggressive wrestling crowds.

"The first time I worked JCW, I stepped through the curtain and was pelted with batteries," says Rick Brady. "It didn't stop until I got back to the back!"

"JCW is a special place," says Mickie Knuckles. "You pretty much have to fight your way out of there."

Puerto Rico has long been known as a dangerous crowd. In his book *The World According to Dutch*, Dutch Mantell chronicles the story of how Glen Jacobs (now Kane in the WWE) saved his life by fighting to and from the ring to save his friend and mentor.

"When I worked with Kevin Sullivan, he told me all these stories about Puerto Rico," says Reed Bentley. "There are boys who sell bags of rocks outside the arenas. The fans buy the rocks to hurl them at the wrestlers."

"Peels Palace had some wild crowds," says Zodiak. "They served beer too, so that made it worse. There were many nights fans jumped in the ring or would 'try' the wrestlers. I remember one night my friend and brother Angel was in the ring having a match, and a guy just kept crossing the line. Finally he bypassed security and got to the ring apron. Angel, wearing motorcross boots, baseball slid him in the face. Put him right out!"

"There has been only one instance where the crowd was more dangerous than the match I was wrestling," says Marc Hauss. "I was wrestling at ECPW in Elmira, New York. The stars must have aligned because when I cut my promo, the fans were furious with me. After the show was over, I was one of the last out of the building. I was getting calls from other wrestlers asking if I had left yet. They warned me not to go outside because there were people waiting for me with tire irons and bats ready to beat the holy hell out of me. The cops provided an escort to my car. That was an interesting night to say the least.

One of the reasons heels often work in groups or factions is so they can be on the lookout for fans who might try something foolish. "Mitch is like me in that he sees everything," says Apollo Garvin. "We don't look at the crowd, but we know where the threats are. When we're at ringside, Mitch will whisper to me, 'Second row, guy in the red shirt.' 'I see him.' You've got to know where those fans are so you can get you and your partner back behind the curtain safe."

Social media has given fans and wrestlers better access to one another outside of the wrestling arena. It's a valuable tool for young wrestlers trying to build a fan base, and it's fun for the fans to get to know their favorite stars a little better. That said, social media has also given the creepier fans more access than ever. Female wrestlers especially are sometimes subject to a little extra attention away from the ring from male fans who don't understand that, as one wrestler put it, accepting a Facebook friend request does not mean they want to sleep with you.

"I've had some creepy messages from fans," says "Crazy" Mary Dobson. "Guys asking for my used ring gear, my socks, stuff like that."

Mary spotted an online post where someone called her a rat, a derogatory term in the wrestling community for someone who sleeps with wrestlers. Mary shrugged it off as she normally does with creepy fans, but a few days later, she got a phone call from the same guy.

"He sounded a little nervous, and he was telling me he was sorry. I wasn't sure why he called, but then I heard Pondo in the background yelling at him. 'Go on! Tell her why you're sorry!' He went over to the guy's house to make him apologize!"

That wasn't the only time Mad Man Pondo had fun at the expense of Mary's admirers. He was sitting in the back at a Shimmer show with Mary's brother watching her compete when they heard two guys in front of them talk about her.

"That 'Crazy' Mary is hot," said one of the fans.

"I know," said the other. "I would totally do her!"

"Aww man, so would I!" said the first.

Pondo laughed to himself, but when Mary's brother nudged him, he knew he had to respond. The old veteran leaned forward between the two fans. "Yeah, 'Crazy' Mary's pretty hot. You think I have a shot with her?"

The two fans turned and got a look at Pondo. "No way," said one of the fans. "You don't stand a chance."

"I don't know," said Pondo. "I think I'm gonna ask her to go home with me tonight."

"No way!" said the fan. "She'd never sleep with you."

"Oh yeah?" said Pondo. "How much money you got? Care to wager twenty bucks on it?"

It was about that point the fans took the hint and realized Pondo was Mary's boyfriend. The bet never happened, but Mary did go home with Pondo that night.

"You get some creepers sometimes," says Lylah Lodge. "Guys who ask for your panty hose. Yes, it happens. I've received cards, letters, poems, and emails. Mostly, you learn to ignore them, because if you answer back, some guys believe they have a chance. Usually if you make a joke of it, make them look silly, they'll leave you alone."

According to Lodge, the creepers aren't near as bad backstage. "Most of the guys I've wrestled with are professionals. In the few cases where someone did say something, it was usually one of the other wrestlers who put them in their place. It also helps having a big, scary boyfriend," she says with a smile.

"When guys get a little creepy with me, I treat them just like any man would," says Mickie. "Although I wish they understood that it is creepy for a male fan to know every detail about your life including things to do with your children."

The vast majority of fans, thankfully, are not creepers, and meeting their favorite performers is a treat for them and the wrestlers.

"It's always so encouraging when I run into fans," says Lylah Lodge. "It's really great when it's people you don't know, especially when I'm on the road. People all over the world watch OVW online, and it makes me happy when people stop to tell me they've enjoyed seeing me.

"I'm constantly amazed when people approach me in public," says Jamin Olivencia. "Especially when I'm on the road. Seems like any time I am in the Atlanta airport, people recognize me. Especially college kids. They watch OVW online, and they're huge fans!"

"I always treat fans with respect, period," says Marc Hauss. "Without the fans I am nothing. So whenever a fan wants to talk, I am there to speak with them or spend time when available."

"Fans help me live my dream on a nightly basis," says Tyson Dux. "Not much of a career if no one is there to love or hate you."

One of the things you discover when you start to meet wrestlers is that the people you hate in the ring are most often the nicest people outside of it. Kenny Ozz, a wrestling fan from Cincinnati, posted this testimonial on the "Baddest Man Alive" Aaron Williams' Facebook page. "Several years ago, a group of friends and I went to an IWI wrestling show in Price Hill. They sold dollar beers at the small, run-down venue, and my crew had a LOT of them. We incessantly heckled every wrestler who came through the curtain. A young kid named Aaron Williams came out for his match, and we let him have it. We asked him if he was the Midget Brock Lesnar. We called him Brock Les-Nerd and Brock Loser. He laughed it off like a pro and put on easily the best match of the night. After the show, he came out and thanked us for coming and said we were funny. Like I said, a true pro, thereby earning my respect. Fast forward a few years, and I am now lucky enough to call Aaron a friend. And he still rules, in and out of the ring. One of the best local wrestlers around and an even better person."

"There's a family that follows me to a lot of shows at different promotions," says Apollo Garvin. "Some places I work heel, some places I work face. Their son is autistic, and for a long time, they had to coach him every night. 'Okay, tonight you cheer Apollo.' Or, 'Okay, tonight you have to boo Apollo.' It worked for a while, but these days he cheers for me no matter what."

"I am always nice to my fans," says frequent heel Mickie Knuckles. "Unless they hate me. Then I am even nicer. Makes them so friggin' mad!!"

Some fans are so passionate about wrestling, they become legends themselves. IWA Mid-South in Southern Indiana is home to a very passionate fan base that leaves an impression on everyone who wrestles there, even those who go on to the WWE.

"I didn't fully understand the depth of the IWA fans until I was signed by OVW," says CM Punk. "I thought these were just local people who decided to come to a wrestling show every week. But I saw the same people at OVW. These were real wrestling fans who had gone to see USWA in the Gardens and later switched to Ian and OVW."

One of the legends of IWA Mid-South was Old Man Charlie. Charlie was either 98 or 103, depending on whether you believe Ian Rotten or Colt Cabana. He sat in the same seat and never missed a show.

When Old Man Charlie passed away, IWA Mid-South honored him with a ten bell salute. This is an honor normally reserved for wrestlers who have passed, though Ian had used it as an angle in the past. When Princess Diana died, they staged a ten bell salute that was interrupted by one of the heels to get heat and lead into the first match. Old Man Charlie's salute was no joke.

"I'm looking around at all these deathmatch guys," says CM Punk, "And it's very serious to them."

Charlie's seat was kept empty as a memorial. A sign was placed on the chair that said, "In Memory of Old Man Charlie." It was sitting vacant with the sign during a double shot weekend. Jerry Lynn was in town and Mike Quackenbush brought some of the first CHIKARA class to town.

On the first night, Colt Cabana and Chris Hero tagged up against Mean and Hard, the tag team of "Mean" Mitch Page & Rollin Hard. Mean and Hard won the match, and afterwards, Cabana turned heel by attacking Chris Hero. He grabbed the microphone and verbally unloaded on Hero, Hero's valet Nadia Nyce, and the fans.

The fans were stunned by the heel turn, but it's what happened next that truly set them off. Cabana went into the crowd, and he sat in Old Man Charlie's chair. Turning on Chris Hero was one thing, but sitting in Old Man Charlie's chair was a bridge too far. Cabana didn't even realize how much he had transgressed until he saw Ian Rotten's wife Patti coming after him. Patti began slapping Cabana, yelling at him to get out of the chair. Security held Patti back, and Cabana escaped any further harm.

Old Man Charlie is gone, but Donna is still around. Donna is the unquestioned wrestling super fan in Louisville and Southern Indiana. Donna does not miss a single show if she can help it. Donna always sits in the front row by the entrance ramp. As a matter of fact, her seat was right next to Old Man Charlie's the night Cabana defiled it.

Donna gets hugs from all the wrestlers, and she's on a first name basis with most of them. I've been to a couple dozen shows in the area over the last year including OVW, IWA Mid-South, EPW, and D1W. The only times I did not see Donna was on a night when someone else had a show across town. Odds are she was at the other show that night.

Donna's been doing this a long, long time. Go back and watch some of the old IWA Mid-South videos with Chris Hero, CM Punk, and Colt Cabana. You will see Donna sitting in the front row by the entrance stealing hugs from everyone.

Fans like Donna and Old Man Charlie are a rare breed, but no matter what their level of mania, all fans are genuinely appreciated. "They are the whole reason we get to do what we do," says Zodiak. "I always take time to respond to things when I can and sign stuff. Give out pictures and so on. I see a lot of guys brush off fans or talk down about them and it bothers me. Without them there would be no wrestling business to enjoy."

"The fans are the ones who pay the money that keeps us in business," says Jamin Olivencia. "I love knowing that what I do entertains and inspires people. It also encourages me to know so many people believe in me."

Professional wrestlers, be they independent or WWE, know that they are nothing without the fans, and most of the time they are happy to say hello, take a picture, or sign an autograph. Just remember to keep your cool, and don't act like a moron, okay?

GETTING PAID

When you're in the ring, you're a star, whether it's in front of fourteen people or seventy-thousand. You become a larger than life character, a hero or a villain idolized and envied by the fans surrounding the ring. The higher up on the card you go, the greater you become, and the glory only compounds once you have a championship belt in your hands.

When the show ends, the fans leave, and the ring is packed away, reality sets in. You are no longer an icon. You're a man or woman who needs to eat. You need shelter and clothing. You need gas in the car. If you have a family, you need to provide for your spouse and children. They have work necessities like gym memberships and wrestling gear, and they have wants like the WWE Network. And if you are a professional wrestler, you will most certainly require medical attention from time to time.

Every pro wrestler dreams of doing what they love full-time, but full-time is much harder to achieve than it was forty years ago. With few exceptions, the independent territories of today do not generate enough money to support a roster of wrestlers full-time. Yes it is possible to wrestle full-time without signing with the WWE, but it's not an easy road.

Even before his run with WWE's NXT as Kassius Ohno, Chris Hero was making a full-time living as a wrestler. His desire to network early on in his career paid dividends, and Hero continues to be in demand at home and around the world. Hero sells T-shirts like most wrestlers, but he also supplements his wrestling income by giving training seminars. He discovered he had an affinity for teaching early in his career, serving as a mentor to guys only a few years behind him in experience and even working as a trainer for Ian Rotten. It's a passion that has served him well, one that can continue to support him when his in-ring career is over.

Colt Cabana is one of the biggest success stories in modern independent wrestling. Colt had a few runs with the WWE, working at developmental schools OVW and Florida Championship Wrestling and on SmackDown, but the WWE brass never "got" Cabana. His greatest fame on the top level came courtesy of his best friend CM Punk, who name-dropped his pal during the 2011 Summer of Punk. "Hey, Colt Cabana!"

Although his TV career never took off, Colt is one of several wrestlers employed to do the motion capture work for WWE video games. Cabana dons the motion capture suit and works on a simulated entrance ramp and in a ring, mimicking the moves of many popular WWE stars. Game creators take this footage and transform Cabana into the WWE stars he copies.

Colt Cabana is also the host of *Art of Wrestling*, one of the very first wrestling podcasts. Cabana was a big fan of Adam Carolla, a pioneer in podcasting comedy. When Colt saw that no one had yet started a wrestling podcast, he created his own. A number of bigger name wrestling stars have since entered the podcast world, most notably Steve Austin, Jim Ross, and Chris Jericho, but Cabana remains one of the most listened to wrestling shows to this day. His show became a primary source of information for this book, as he spends a great deal of time talking to independent wrestling stars like Chris Hero, Adam Cole, and Cherry Bomb.

Cabana is a hustler who stays on the road constantly, bringing boxes of t-shirts and other merchandise along for the ride. He's built an empire out of the Colt Cabana brand, and he's a draw just about everywhere he wrestles. Cabana has also produced two documentaries about life on the road, and he also does stand up. He's worked the big name promotions, from Ring of Honor to Pro Wrestling Guerilla, but he's not so big he won't go back and work for the little guys who helped along the way.

Hero and Cabana are the exception rather than the rule in today's wrestling business. Many of today's wrestlers, including main event talent and title holders, hold regular jobs. Hy Zaya works in a liquor store. Ian Rotten works fast food. Lylah Lodge works as a massage therapist. Mickie Knuckles and Zodiak not only have day jobs, but are taking college classes.

Mad Man Pondo has a regular day job when he's not on the road, but back in the late 1990s he stumbled into a very unique opportunity. He started his own public access talk show on cable, a show that featured nudity and obscene language. His show caught the attention of the producers of *The Jerry Springer Show*.

Pondo was cast as a guest on the show. He made two different appearances playing different guests on the program. Yes, folks, shocking as it may be, The *Jerry Springer Show* is all a work!

Pondo was such a hit, the producers asked if he could recommend other people for the show. "They love interesting people, and they knew I knew plenty. It turned into a regular gig for me. I was one of their go-to casting agents, making $600-800 a week. The problem with Springer is they wanted you on call all the time," he says. "It got to be too much, trying to wrestle and casting the show, so I eventually quit."

That's the challenge for those who work other jobs. Despite the obvious benefits like health insurance. life is a constant balancing act, working their schedules around booking opportunities. Most are lucky enough to have understanding bosses who are willing to work with them on their travel schedules. Those who don't usually quit and look for a new job that will give them the flexibility they need.

The full-time wrestlers are true riverboat gamblers. They depend on their gimmick table sales and they live at the mercy of promoters, who are not always dependable when it comes to paying their wrestlers.

"Sometimes you travel a long way for a show, and you get stiffed," says Jamin Olivencia. "The promoter doesn't pay, and you have to call your family to ask them to wire you some money. It's frustrating, but that's when it really pays to have a family who believes in you."

Apollo Garvin was once paid $75 for an appearance, all in quarters. "I poured them out and counted them on the hood of the promoter's car," he says. "It was all there, but I was mad!"

DJ Hyde makes his full-time living as a wrestler and the owner of CZW. Being the owner means he not only has his own living to worry about, but the livelihoods of his wrestlers. Hyde has already done much to increase CZW's audience and profitability, expanding CZW from a hardcore promotion to include a broader range of wrestling styles, but he finds himself doing a constant balancing act as he tries to keep his business profitable while making his workers happy.

The biggest challenge for Hyde is making the tough choices creatively and doing what's best for business. Hyde has to keep the long term story and success of CZW first and foremost, but that goal often conflicts with the desires of the individual wrestlers. "CZW wrestlers are my family and my best friends. That means they're not just my employees; they all know how to work me to get what they want.

"Case in point, one of my top female stars has a match this coming weekend with me. She wants to do her usual spots and put herself over big, but I see the big picture, not just this match, but the next few months of matches. She's never faced a guy my size, and realistically, she can't just go toe to toe with me and be believable. She won't like it, but she's going to have to struggle, to take an underdog role. It's not her way, but it make things more believable and get the fans behind her."

"I always heard guys like Les Thatcher and Al Snow tell me what the wrestling business really was," says Hyde. "I never understood their lessons fully until I became the owner of CZW."

One of the best ways wrestlers can supplement their pay from promoters is the gimmick table. In the world of professional wrestling, a gimmick is anything the wrestler sells to make some extra money, from autographed photos to T-shirts to anything else you can imagine.

"I want more than wrestling fans wanting my gear," says Eric Emanon. "I want a design that doesn't scream 'wrestling shirt' when you look at it. They usually sell pretty damn quick too. Luckily I have a friend who has a multi-screen press machine for t-shirts so I can get my shirts for a pretty good deal and I'm able to sell them at a small profit. But at the same time, all the money goes back in for more merchandise.

"I come up with all my merchandise," says LuFisto. "I'm a graphic designer by profession so I design my t-shirts, website, 8x10 pictures, and so on. I've heard stuff about panty hose and underwear being sold, but I've never seen it. It did sign a butt cheek once!"

Mickie Knuckles designs her own gimmicks as well. "I am in college right now for graphic design so I am artistically inclined. I usually make money on the gimmick table, but I have a soft spot for children so I end up giving most away."

Menace offers a variety of gimmicks on his table. "I sell 8x10 photos, buttons, cups, stickers, anything I can get my face or logo on, if I can sell it then I'm making money."

Marc Hauss is always on the lookout for new ideas. "If I ever see a catchphrase or logo that strikes an idea, I write it down. For the most part almost all of my merchandise ideas are flukes of seeing something or someone says; something that strikes a chord with me."

Hauss sells a variety of merchandise including, T-shirts, custom sunglasses, 8x10 photos, trucker hats, wristbands, and backpacks. "I have searched the internet for countless hours for good pricing and quality work. Also through constant networking I have been able to find good quality people running some great quality mom and pop shops willing to work with me. I'm at the point where I have a company sponsoring me to wear their clothing and become a reseller of their merchandise."

Hauss has also witnessed some creative selling at the tables in his time. "I saw a wrestler take a guy's own hat, sign it, and sell it back to him! I've also seen wrestlers sell hugs, and a chance to arm-wrestle."

Zodiak mostly designs his own gimmicks, but he's also taken ideas from fans. "I've been blessed to have friends and fans send random works and ideas for shirts, pictures and other items. I want to work on DVDs and fan packages soon."

Tyson Dux also relies on the fans for new ideas. "There are fans out there who are by far the most creative people. They send me stuff just for me, and I will ask them if I could use it."

Lylah Lodge offers the usual merchandise like t-shirts at her table, but she also offers something a little special. "I make cupcakes," she says. "I bake them and decorate them myself to sell at the shows."

Wrestlers today have some great resources for making gimmicks such as Prowrestlingtees.com, a spin-off of onehourtees.com. Not only can fans buy these shirts at live events, they can go online to get apparel from indie stars like Colt Cabana, LuFisto, Chris Hero, the Young Bucks, and Cliff Compton as well as legends like Kamala, Jake "The Snake" Roberts, and "Hacksaw" Jim Duggan.

Regardless of whether a person intends to be a full-time wrestler or not, most veterans, from Mick Foley to Roddy Piper to Jim Cornette advise aspiring wrestlers to get their college education. Having that education gives you a fall back if wrestling doesn't work out or if you need a break. What's more, having a college degree can make you a better negotiator and business person on the wrestling circuit, as Ricky Morton of the Rock 'n Roll Express points out.

"The promoters robbed us," says Ricky, referring to himself and his tag partner Robert Gibson. The Rock 'n Roll Express sold out arenas, but they were never paid as much as the top singles stars of their day. "I have no one to blame but Ricky Morton for that. I didn't have that education, so I had no idea they were taking advantage of me. I don't say that because I want something. I say that so that other people will be smarter than we were."

When you're a full-time wrestler, every penny helps, especially when you're depending on those pennies to get you back home. It's a day to day struggle, but for those who dream of nothing but wrestling, it's a struggle they gladly face. As Ron Mathis put it, "As long as I have food for me and food for my dog, I'm doing okay."

Ron Mathis wears his happy face against Dustin Rayz.
(Photo courtesy Marked Out Photography.)

"SOMETHING IS WRONG…"

It was just after 11 PM. I had spent a good hour and a half hearing stories from Mad Man Pondo and "Crazy" Mary Dobson at Applebees. We were discussing the WWE and the WWE Network as we were leaving when NXT, the WWE's training show, came up.

"You keep up with NXT?" asked Mary. "Is it true what I heard about Sami?"

Sami is Sami Callihan, known to fans of NXT as Solomon Crowe. A few days earlier a story broke on the Internet that Callahan broke his leg at a house show. It's the worst kind of news any wrestler can have, made even worse by the timing. Injuries are an unpleasant fact of life in professional wrestling. Say what you will about wrestling being "fake" or "staged," these men and women take great risks with their bodies every night they step in the ring. Most of them do it without the benefit of health insurance.

Let me repeat that last part: most of them do it without the benefit of health insurance!

Even at the top level, WWE, wrestlers are not provided with medical insurance. Wrestlers are left with a few options: setting money aside in savings; taking on a side job that provides medical insurance; or praying to God that they are not critically injured. There are men and women who follow all three options, and most follow more than one.

"I love Obamacare," says Reed Bentley with a smile. Bentley is 23, and under the Affordable Care Act is covered by his parents' insurance for another three years. Bentley has suffered a few concussions, but has been lucky not to sustain any major injury thus far in his career. That's not a small feat, considering Bentley has spent much of that time working for Ian Rotten in IWA Mid-South.

Mad Man Pondo spent a number of years working for Rotten and other hardcore promoters. He has the scars to prove it. Years ago, Pondo suffered a fractured skull while working in the ring. He was without health insurance and had no money, so in true hardcore style, he super glued his skull back together. The same evening we discussed Sami Callihan's broken leg, Pondo had me feel the ridge where he personally repaired his skull.

Pondo has numerous scars and marks across his face and body from years of deathmatches. He took a light tube tied to a baseball bat across his left temple from Reed Bentley that required twelve stitches, and he tore his rotator cuff. "You don't realize how much you use that until you try to get out of bed without it," says Pondo.

"Crazy" Mary has a few scars of her own. "I think Ron Mathis has stapled my tongue more than anyone else," she says with a laugh. "I also once let Ludark Shaitan give me a mohawk with wooden skewers." Mary is as fearless as anyone in a deathmatch, but Mad Man Pondo has urged her to be more cautious. "She can't get herself all scarred up if she wants to get to the next level."

Apollo Garvin has suffered seven concussions in twenty years. His knees are shot, but he's still able to run a 5K in addition to his ring work. He considers himself lucky he's had no broken bones, but every morning he wakes up with severe muscle spasms. "They shake the whole bed," he says. "My wife calls it her alarm clock. When the bed starts shaking, it's usually time to get up."

Wrestlers work hard to protect themselves and each other, but sometimes a slip up can occur even between people who know each other inside and out. Aaron Williams received a concussion courtesy of his long time travel buddy Sami Callihan when Callihan positioned him wrong for a piledriver. "The next thing I remember is crawling backstage," Williams recalls. "I made it through the curtain, grabbed a garbage can, and regurgitated.

"One of the boys asked me the last thing I remember. I said it was taking the piledriver from Sami. The guy told me, 'You wrestled another fifteen minutes after that.' I couldn't believe it, but I went on auto-pilot for fifteen minutes. I still have no memory of that match."

Concussions are one of the most common injuries among wrestlers, and their impact in the short and long term can be scary. Austin Bradley was working a three way match with Dale Patricks and Anthony Lee when he suffered a concussion. They were attempting a Tower of Doom spot with Austin on top when he was pushed out of the ring to the floor. He broke his wrist and hit his head in the fall. Several wrestlers raced to the ring to check him out. Austin managed to get back in the ring and finish the match with a diving headbutt.

"I made it to the back," says Austin. "Randy Terrez came up and asked if I was okay. I looked down, saw I had my wrestling gear on, and asked if it was time for my match. Then I tried to find Patricks and Lee to go over match. I had no memory that the match ever took place. The only reason I know what happened is because I watched it back on video."

Tyson Dux has suffered multiple concussions, shoulder separations, broken fingers, and broken toes. He also had a torn ACL, a torn bicep, and a cut above his left eye. "The cut was so bad, you could see my skull. I got twenty-five stitches for that beauty." Dux also suffered a knee injury that put him on the shelf for a year and may have also cost him a WWE contract.

Fortunately for Dux, Canada has free healthcare for all its citizens, so paying for medical bills has never been an issue. "Most of the time I was injured in Canada so I could get fixed up under my health care. The times I've been hurt in the States, I've been able to drag myself home before getting repaired."

Wrestling both men and women has taken its toll on Lylah Lodge. Her list of injuries includes a cracked orbital bone, trouble with discs in her neck, a hand injury, a shoulder dislocation, and two cracked ribs.

Ron Mathis has a similar list of maladies, from a knot floating in the small of his back, to a scar on his palm from a gash that wasn't properly stitched, to a left elbow swollen the size of a tennis ball. Despite the obvious issues, Mathis refuses to see a doctor. "I know what he's gonna say. Stop wrestling. That ain't gonna happen."

In 2013 LuFisto suffered a very serious injury on a live Internet pay-per-view for women's promotion Shimmer. She climbed the corner to do a moonsault on one of her opponents and noticed that no one was in the right position. She climbed down and kicked one of the other girls, hoping they would move. LuFisto climbed back to the top of the corner and didn't notice that no one had moved until she was in the air.

LuFisto tried hard to land safely, but she crashed hard to the floor, lower body first. She took a second to check herself out, making sure her head, hands, and arms were not injured. She pushed up with her right leg, which hurt but was fine, but when she put her weight on her left leg, she knew something was wrong. She struggled to finish her part of the match and made her way to the back.

LuFisto had an exploded knee cap. The knee cap had literally broken into four pieces, and her doctor scheduled her for surgery immediately. After telling her doctor how the injury happened, the doctor laughed. "And a broken knee cap is all you have?"

DJ Hyde has doctors on staff at CZW for himself and his wrestlers. He has never suffered any broken bones, but when he is injured, he accepts the pain as part of the job. "Everything in the ring is real to an extent," he says. "You can do everything perfectly 99% of the time. Then 1% something happens.

"Being injured is part of the game. If I don't wake up every day in pain, something is wrong."

When I sat down to interview Hy Zaya, he was still suffering the effects of a hard bump from Chase Stevens more than two weeks earlier. Hy Zaya has had his share of injuries, but he credits prayer with keeping him in relatively good health. "As a young guy without medical insurance, I pray to stay well a lot. I really think prayer is a big reason why I haven't been more hurt."

Injuries are a fact of life in professional wrestling. If you wrestle, you will get hurt. If there's a bright side to that unfortunate fact, it's that every injury opens an opportunity for someone else. Shortly after LuFisto underwent surgery for her exploded knee, she was able to choose her replacement in a match against Japanese star Sumie Sakai. LuFisto convinced Sakai to offer her opponent a falls count anywhere, no rules match. Only then did she tell Sakai that her opponent was LuFisto's doll manager, Pegaboo. Pegaboo hit the Japanese vet with the Head Butt of Death and scored a pin fall.

"Beware of Pegaboo," says LuFisto. "She's one tough bitch!"

"Crazy" Mary Dobson and Mad Man Pondo. Aren't they adorable?
(Photo courtesy Michael Herm Photography.)

FAMILY

One of the first people I interviewed for this project was Jamin Olivencia. After exchanging numbers at OVW one night, we made plans to do a phone interview on a Tuesday night around 11 PM. Shortly after 11 that night, I got a message from Jamin on Facebook. "Sorry, will call soon. Being a parent."

Turns out it was the night before the first day of school for Jamin's daughter, the love of his life. She was too excited to sleep, and Daddy was doing everything he could to make sure she got some rest. We ended up talking the next night, and yes, we did talk fatherhood in addition to wrestling.

"It's hard," Jamin admits. "You make a lot of sacrifices in this business, and that includes time that could be spent with her. I don't have another job. Wrestling is my full time job. I make money off my T-shirts and pay offs, so I have to keep working.

"Still, I know that she understands why I do what I do, and she's inspired by that. I tell her all the time, 'You are the creator of your own world. You can be whatever you like.' I want her to follow her dream like I did."

Fans and friends who follow Olivencia on Facebook know that he makes the most of his time with his daughter. It's not uncommon to see him post photos of the two clowning around and having fun in their moments together.

Olivencia's not the only one raising a child while pursuing his dream. Apollo Garvin has a wife and two daughters. He enjoys the full support of his immediate family, but he admits it's a struggle being gone as much as he is. "I've missed anniversaries, birthdays, Christmases, Thanksgivings and other holidays. My wife and girls understand, but it's never fun having to leave a family function in the middle to drive four hours to a show."

Aaron Williams credits two things for keeping him grounded: his faith and his wife. He's a devoted Christian, and his faith helps to keep his marriage strong. He and his wife Brittany don't have children, but he enjoys the time he gets with his nieces and nephews.

"It's hard to miss family time, which usually happens on the weekends when I am on the road. But my family understands. This is my full-time job. I don't have anything else. I'm thankful for their support."

"Crazy" Mary Dobson enjoys the full support of her mentor, best friend, and fiancé, Mad Man Pondo. Now 21 and 45 respectively, Mary and Pondo hit it off shortly after she started training with Mickie Knuckles. They've been together ever since.

Meeting Mary has made Pondo into a new man as well. He's taking fewer ridiculous bumps than he used to, and he's also in the best shape of his life. By doing away with sodas, eating organic, and walking three and a half miles a day, Pondo shed more than 60 pounds and dropped two T-shirt sizes. He wants to keep on living a long while, wrestling and enjoying life with his girl.

Cherry Bomb was also lucky enough to find love on the independent wrestling circuit. She and her husband Pepper Parks met years ago, but it wasn't until they both wound up in Japan at the same time they really connected. "I saw a Facebook post that said he was in Japan," says Cherry. "I sent him a message that said, 'Hey! You speak English, I speak English. Let's go to Sizzler!" Their friendship grew into something more over time, and in 2014, they were married.

Not everyone has the benefit of a significant other on the road or at home, but many wrestlers, single or not, still have at least one family member they can count on: Mom.

"I love my mom," says Adam Cole. "She's my best friend, and she's always there for me."

Cherry Bomb's mother is her best friend and has been her biggest fan since day one. Not only did she go to training with her daughter, she bought her a weight bench, telling her, "You need to put some muscle on, honey!" She also makes a point to buy something from every wrestler who has a table when she goes to shows so that everyone gets at least a little extra money.

Colt Cabana's mom wanted to go a step further. "She always wanted to hang out with the other wrestling moms!" Mama Cabana was disappointed when she learned that wrestling moms didn't group like Little League parents. Still, she supported her son, and even baked snacks for him to take for the class when he was in training.

If there's one thing sweeter than a Mom, it's a Grandmother. Hy Zaya's one of the most serious and stoic of wrestlers, but ask him about his grandma, and the Hood Ninja melts. "She's my queen," he says. "She is the feistiest woman in the world. She's a real life Madea. I don't know that she approves of my wrestling, but I know she's happy for me. She's also the only one in my family besides my brothers who's seen me wrestle."

Susie, as Hy Zaya calls her, continues to inspire her grandson in and out of the ring. At age seventy-five she is currently in school, working on her college diploma. She's a deeply spiritual woman, and her devotion to God rubbed off on Hy Zaya.

"Early on, she told me to remember that we wrestle not against flesh and blood," says Hy Zaya, referring to the scripture in Ephesians 6. "Because of her, I started to pray every night before my matches. I begin with the Lord's Prayer. Then I ask the Lord to protect me and my opponent from pain and injury, asking him to preserve us so we walk out in the same good health as we enter. Then I thank him for giving me the opportunity to do what I love."

Prayer proved to be the connecting point between Hy Zaya and a few other young wrestlers. OVW did a few crossover shows with EPW in 2013, and both Jamin Olivencia and Paredyse were part of the OVW "invasion."

"They were the first two guys who ever prayed with me in the locker room," says Hy Zaya. "That night we became brothers."

That's one of the best parts of being a wrestler, the unique brotherhood and/or sisterhood that connects you with those who share your passion. Those who wrestle together and travel together form a unique bond that will never be broken. Not everyone has a spouse or children or even parents they can rely on, but no one who lives for the squared circle is ever alone. They are family.

WWE

A lot of wrestlers will tell you they never had any ambitions of wrestling with WWE. A lot of wrestlers are terrible, terrible liars. "Guys who say they never wanted to work for WWE are guys who wanted to but have come to realize they never will," says Mad Man Pondo.

Despite the ups and downs of its programming, WWE is the number one, undisputed top promotion in the world. Despite their denials, the vast majority of indie wrestlers keep up with number one. Aaron Williams, for instance, is very public about his fandom. Not only does he post about the current product, he frequently posts about watching past WWE events on the WWE Network.

Forty years ago you could have made a very good living at any number of promotions across the country if you worked hard enough. Today, very few wrestlers are able to do what they love full-time outside WWE. When Vince McMahon, Jr., took power from his father, he began cherry picking the top talent from the AWA, Mid-Atlantic Wrestling, WCCW, CWA, and other regional promotions. Over time the regionals folded, leaving WWE as the last man standing.

Ironically, WWE not only killed off the territory system, but their greatest source for new talent. WWE realized their error and attempted to correct it by creating their own farm territories. Ohio Valley Wrestling in Louisville and Heartland Wrestling Association in Cincinnati were the first. Then came Steve Keirn's Florida Championship Wrestling, followed by the current farm club, NXT. But even NXT remains dependent on the independents in its search for new talent. That's why WWE frequently invites indie wrestlers to participate in its television productions as extras. They get a chance to meet WWE hopefuls and even give them tryouts while filling the extra roles on the show.

Monday night, September 1, 2014 was a big night for Southern Indiana wrestling fans and wrestlers. Like other fans and wrestlers across the country, most of them were tuned in to Monday Night Raw. All of a sudden, with no warning and no introduction, a familiar face appeared on screen! She was given no name and little mention except for being the Miz's personal makeup artist, but fans of indie wrestling knew immediately that was no run of the mill extra.

"'Crazy' Mary Dobson is on Raw!"

"That's no makeup girl! That's 'Crazy' Mary!"

"Forget the Miz, put 'Crazy' Mary in the ring!"

Three days later, I sat in Applebees with "Crazy" Mary and Mad Man Pondo as she recounted her experience on Raw. "I was invited to be at Raw and SmackDown for a tryout, so I flew in to Kansas City on Sunday and met up with Heather Patera. We drove to Des Moines the next day. I had flown in on Spirit, so I only had one carry on with the outfits they told me to bring and my workout gear.

"When I got there, they said they would be holding tryouts on Tuesday in Nebraska. Only problem was, Nebraska requires you to have a license, and I didn't have time to go through the licensing process. But then John Laurinitis came out and said they would be doing tryouts that day, so I got my tryout in Des Moines after all!"

It wasn't easy keeping her WWE visit a secret. A week earlier, her mother leaked the news on Facebook in a post that was quickly deleted. Mary's appearance caught most of her fans and peers by surprise, but no one was more surprised than she when she checked Twitter and Facebook.

"I couldn't believe how excited everyone was. It wasn't like I got to wrestle, but everyone was so supportive."

Mary had high praise for the Miz, who made sure the aspiring Diva got as much face time as she could get during the segment. So successful was he, Mary had to wear a mask the next night on Smackdown when she appeared as a Rosebud in Adam Rose's Exotic Express entourage.

Mary also made sure to say hello to one of Pondo's old friends. "Pondo worked with Kane way back in the day when he was first starting out. He hadn't been in touch with him for years, not since he made it to WWE, but he told me I should take a chance and say hello. I finally mustered the courage to stop him and say, 'Hi, Kane, I'm Sarah. I'm Pondo's girl.' Kane broke out in a big smile. He was so nice."

Mary was invited back a few weeks later for the post Night of Champions episode of Raw in Memphis. This time Mary's partner in crime Pondo got to tag along. Pondo never had any aspirations of going to the WWE; his main goal when he set out was to wrestle in Japan, which he did 42 times. On September 22, in Memphis he and Mary were part of the Exotic Express. Mary dressed as Pocahontas, and Pondo wore a sombrero. "I didn't get to keep it," he says. "WWE property!"

Another wrestler who got the call for a tryout at TV is Aaron Williams, although he nearly missed out on his chance. "I was sitting home watching TV with my wife on a Thursday night," says Aaron Williams, recalling his first real brush with the WWE. "I always screen my phone calls, and when my phone rang, it came up as a Connecticut number. I showed it to my wife and said, 'Look, honey, Vince McMahon is calling me!'"

Williams let the call go to voice mail and forgot all about it. On Sunday, he finally got around to checking the message. It was a woman from WWE, offering him a tryout before Raw the very next day in Pittsburgh. Williams began calling and texting, frantically trying to reach the WWE representative. He just knew he had blown his one chance at WWE.

Williams was working another job at the time. When he got off work at 11 AM Monday, he called his dad to talk about the missed opportunity. That was when the woman from WWE finally responded. She told him they had filled his slot but that it had come open again. He could still try out, but he had to be in Pittsburgh at 2 PM. "I told her I was in Cincinnati, and there was no way I could get there by two. She said to get there as fast as I could."

Williams arrived in Pittsburgh at 5 PM. After changing into his ring gear and getting checked out by a trainer, he waited for an hour, only to be told the tryouts were over. "I was disappointed, but I got the news from William Regal. I'm a big Regal mark, and to hear Regal talk to me and the other boys, that was cool."

Williams got to hang out backstage that night with his old pal Jon Moxley, who was in the early part of his run with the Shield as Dean Ambrose. At Midnight, he was told he could try out the next day in his hometown of Cincinnati. "I left at Midnight, got home at 6 AM, slept for an hour, got up, and headed down to the arena, where I finally got my tryout."

WWE auditions the hopefuls both in the ring and in front of the camera, although the camera is sometimes nothing more than a prop. Wrestlers who have received the invite usually find themselves in a "hurry up and wait" situation, being staged in one room and then another as they anticipate their time to shine. Tryouts are first and foremost in their minds, but WWE staffers are focused almost solely on the evening's television taping.

When the time does come to audition, wrestlers are herded into rooms - sometimes individually, sometimes in groups - to cut promos for talent scouts like the Brooklyn Brawler and William Regal. If time allows, wrestlers are invited to do tryout matches in the ring. A few lucky wrestlers, like Colt Cabana and Jamin Olivencia, get to work dark matches in front of the live crowd.

Auditioning for WWE is a high pressure endeavor. For every one person who gets the opportunity, there are dozens on the outside who would kill to take their spot. Staying patient and keeping a cool head is critical, as it only takes one little mistake to blow your chances.

"I missed my chance because told off the wrong guy," says DJ Hyde. "They offered me a contract and took it back the same day. You don't tell off one of Vince McMahon's number two guys and get hired." Hyde has since patched up his differences with WWE. Now, when WWE is in town, Hyde is one of the guys they call to supply extras from his CZW roster.

Another favorite source for extra talent is Ohio Valley Wrestling. It's been years since OVW was the official training territory for WWE, but the school still enjoys a strong reputation for those who want to make it to WWE. The school continues to attract top prospects like Lylah Lodge.

"My boyfriend and I were in a bad car accident," says Lylah. "We won a settlement, somewhere around ten grand, and we spent it on traveling to Louisville."

Lylah and her boyfriend Dash Sullivan (the kayfabe nephew of Kevin Sullivan) attended a WWE tryout at OVW. "John Laurinitis was there, and he seemed to like me," says Lylah. "The first day was a lot of training, and the goal was to make it to the three on three matches on the second day. I was one of only six ladies to make it to the second day."

Lylah didn't get her WWE break during that tryout, but she loved her time at OVW so much, she vowed to become a student. When money allowed, she and Sullivan moved to Louisville to train with Rip Rogers and Danny Davis.

"The only brushes I had with WWE were in my OVW days," says Mitchell Huff. "The WWE scouts would come down to watch us regularly. I was pulled aside by three or four of them, and they all said something along the lines of, 'Stick with this, kid. You got it. You will get a contract in a year.' I didn't stick with it when I was young, and I still regret it. I wonder where I'd be now if I hadn't walked away."

Jamin Olivencia made his first appearance as a WWE extra when he was only nineteen. "It's like a homecoming for me," he says. "I worked with so many of the guys who are there now when they were at OVW. They're always glad to see me, and most of them are like, 'Why aren't you here already with us?'"

Olivencia has made multiple appearances for WWE over the years. He's had dark matches and televised matches as a jobber, most notably as one of Ryback's early victims, Nick Nardone. In 2014 he made a few appearances as a Rosebud, part of Adam Rose's entourage. He also had a run-in with the unhinged Alicia Fox, who pushed his face into a plate of food backstage.

"The Rosebud bit was so cool," said Jamin, whose passion and energy were on full display as part of the Exotic Express. "They actually put me in charge of the group that night. I've been around so much, they know they can trust me in spots like that."

Olivencia would love to make the main roster one day, but he's appreciative of the time he's had on the big stage and makes the most of every opportunity. He also has a great relationship with the bosses. "Stephanie and Hunter are always very kind and gracious."

"I think I have the record for a guy not under contract making the most appearances on WWE," says Tyson Dux. "They used me every month for two years straight, from 2002 to 2004. I even had my own entrance music."

Dux was around so often, Stephanie McMahon and the others thought he was already in their developmental system. Dux kept asking for a deal, and McMahon finally agreed to meet with him and John Laurinitis one night after Raw. That night, before the meeting could take place, Dux blew out his knee in a match against Mark Jindrak.

"Dean Malenko helped me to the back," he said. "I was leaning against some production crates, waiting to see the trainer, when Johnny Ace (Laurinitis) came up and put his arm around me. 'Tough break, kid,' he said. I knew then I wasn't getting signed."

It was bad timing, but Dux, who has fully recovered from his injury, looks back on his experience fondly. "It's awesome to see how organized and professional everything is. It's not a small set up in the slightest but it shows how years of experience and insane amount of hard work has got them to where they are."

Everyone aspires to get a WWE contract, but as Chris Hero learned, getting the contract is not enough to guarantee you will make it. Hero struggled with his weight for many years, but when he finally developed a trimmer, more WWE style body, he got his shot. He was sent to NXT in Florida, and he was renamed Kassius Ohno. He had a solid following, and he had a very good run feuding with William Regal. Then in November of 2013 he was released from his contract.

Many theories abound as to why Hero was let go. Some said he didn't have the discipline for conditioning WWE wanted. Some said he wasn't as willing to conform to the WWE "style." Whatever the reason, Hero has kept mum. He knows his window of opportunity is far from closed, but rather than dwell on what went wrong, he chose to press on. Hero was back on the independent circuit in a matter of weeks and made a snowy return to his old stomping grounds of IWA Mid-South.

Persistence is the key to getting noticed and getting your break, though persistence can work against you if you're working the wrong person. "I heard Terry Taylor say in an interview once that he had called Pat Patterson every day for five years before getting a job," says Cherry Bomb. "Somehow I got hold of the phone number for Ty Bailey, one of the talent relations people at WWE. I took Terry's advice, and I started calling. After six months he finally booked me for a tryout and extra work. After the show I kept on calling him, every Tuesday and Thursday, but I always got his voice mail. Then one day he answered. He didn't say hi; he just said my name. He gave me a huge tongue lashing for calling him as much as I did. I knew I was toast, but thankfully he's not with WWE any more. I've got a clean slate!"

For independent wrestlers of today, the WWE is the golden ticket. In the modern era it is your best shot at making a full-time living as a pro wrestler. Just working a WWE show is a memorable experience, even for those who know they will never be a star on that stage.

"I've been the bunny three times," says DJ Hyde, referring to the infamous bunny who accompanied Adam Rose's Exotic Express. "Two hundred fifty bucks a night to be the bunny."

Nice work if you can get it.

"IF I CAN BE SERIOUS FOR A MINUTE..."

Prior to the rise of the WWF in the 1980s the country was divided into a number of wrestling territories. The territories were each run by promoters who had come up through the business, and every region had its own unique style and flavor. The WWF squashed the old territory system by taking wrestling national. They raided the top talent from all the regionals, and eventually the regionals went under.

Fast forward to today, and you'll find there are more promotions and territories than even in the glory years of the National Wrestling Alliance. Independent wrestling is everywhere, in arenas, high school gyms, warehouses, bowling alleys, former storefronts, and roller rinks. In some parts of the country you can see independent wrestling two and three times a week, every week, if you know where to go and where to look.

There's no shortage of outlets for people who want to see live wrestling, but the ubiquity of independent wrestling is both good and bad. As DJ Hyde of CZW puts it, "There are too many promotions and too few promoters who know what they are doing."

In New Jersey where the CZW home arena is, there are five smaller promotions running in the same area. Not one of them is run by a person with any real experience in professional wrestling. They were not trained by anyone, and they never shadowed any promoters. They were fans or self-taught wrestlers who decided to open their own promotions.

"Guys like that don't know how to promote," says Hyde. "They book names and make matches, but they don't know how to tell stories and create angles that sell tickets."

That may sound like professional snobbery, but there's a valid point to Hyde's lament. There's something to be said for professional wrestling to be scarce and regulated while wrestlers are required to be trained and licensed. Scarcity fosters demand. It also forces promoters to be choosy about who they book, allowing the cream to rise faster. Licensing promotes accountability. It gives the wrestlers peace of mind they are working with true professionals. It can also ensure the fans are getting a quality product in the ring.

Across the river from my hometown is Ohio Valley Wrestling, one of the most successful and respected wrestling schools and indie territories of the last twenty years. OVW is licensed by the state of Kentucky. Kentucky also requires anyone who steps beyond the barriers that surround the ring to be licensed. That means wrestlers, ring announcers, referees, and even time keepers are required to pay a license fee and be subject to random drug testing.

Kentucky also has very strict rules about blood in matches. These rules came about in the late 1990s, when complaints about excessive blood and violence at IWA Mid-South caused the Kentucky State Athletic Commission to step in and set some boundaries.

"The blood rule in Kentucky used to be called the Pondo/Rotten law," says Mad Man Pondo, who rolls his eyes at the dubious honor.

Promotions are far and few between in Kentucky. The closest promotion to OVW is Southern Wrestling Entertainment in Shepherdsville, twenty miles to the south. Kentucky keeps close tabs on the number of promoters in the state and the number of wrestlers who wrestle there. They don't want too many promotions in one area, and they want everyone to be licensed and legal.

On my side of the river in Indiana it's a completely different story. In the 1960s Indiana changed the way it regulated professional wrestling. Dick the Bruiser, the legendary grappler and promoter from Indianapolis, went before the State Assembly and convinced them wrestling was theater and not sport. To paraphrase, if Bruiser wanted to stick a pencil in someone's eye in the ring, that was between him and the other artist in the ring, and not an Athletic Commissioner.

In 2014 no less than four promotions were running weekly or monthly shows in Clark County Indiana, right across the river from Louisville. Some of the wrestlers in the promotions were trained, a few of them by OVW. Some were long time veterans with decades of experience not only in small territories but international groups in Japan, and Mexico. Some were self-taught, backyard brawlers who, like every other professional wrestler in the country, dreamed of clawing their way to the top.

States like Kentucky take a lot of flack from promoters and wrestlers who resent any government interference in their work. However, licensing promoters gives the state some power to make sure that the people running wrestling promotions in their state know what they are doing and do everything in an ethical manner - or as ethical as they can in the wrestling business.

This may come as a shock, but the wrestling business is still filled with shady, disreputable individuals who will do anything to get ahead and make an extra buck. What's more, there are many promoters out there willing to go to great lengths to deprive their rivals of that same opportunity.

One long time indie veteran recalled a story about his old boss when another promotion tried to run in his town. "[The new promoter] plastered the city with posters, and it looked like they were going to draw a big crowd. The night of the show, no one came. The doors opened, and no one was there. It took them about an hour to discover that we were out on the street near the entrance to the parking lot, turning people away and telling them the show was canceled."

States that regulate wrestling are better able to respond to incidents like these. They give fans a voice to advocate for a quality product, and the wrestlers an ally against being cheated.

What's more, licensing also gives the workers some peace of mind about the people they work with. When a wrestler steps in the ring, they are essentially putting their bodies in the hands of their opponents. Just as none of us would want to go under the knife with an inexperienced doctor, most wrestlers prefer to step in the ring with someone who has had the proper training.

"Working the independent scene is a lot like having a blind date every night," says Ricky Morton, who still tags with Robert Gibson as the Rock 'n Roll Express in addition to working as a single. "When a young guy comes to me and asks what I want to do, the first thing I tell them is, 'Don't hurt me.'"

While there are exceptions to every rule, backyard brawlers tend to be, by nature, more dangerous. They are self-taught, having copied their move sets off television, and their lack of formal training makes them far more likely to cause injury to themselves and others. Licensing and required training promotes a safer work environment for all involved.

A safer work environment also creates a better product, especially in professional wrestling. When wrestlers have the training and the know-how to work safely, they are better able to perform in the ring. It doesn't mean they take fewer risks; it only means the risks are more calculated. Wrestlers know they can trust one another to keep each other safe, and that gives them more freedom to put on the matches that makes us cheer.

So if licensing promotes a better product, does that mean that all unlicensed promotions and wrestlers are inferior? Certainly not! There are many seasoned, responsible promoters running wrestling promotions in states that do not require any licensing. There are many unlicensed but well-trained wrestlers working shows for whomever is willing to book them, giving their all on the mat every night. And there are plenty of licensed promoters and licensed wrestlers who have no business being involved in professional wrestling, no matter what their state regulators may say.

    Having a license to promote wrestling does not make you a great promoter any more than not having a license makes you a bad one. Like many things in life, it's buyer beware when you decide where to spend your money to see wrestling.

Adam Cole and "War Beard" Hanson.
(Photo courtesy Ichiban Drunk.)

GETTING YOUR FIX

Now that the messy discussion about licensing and outlaws is out of the way, let's get to a much more important question. Where can you get a better look at today's independent wrestlers?

An easy transition from the world of WWE to the world of independent wrestling is via the larger indie promotions, starting right at the top with Ring of Honor. Founded in 2001, ROH owes its birth to the death of the legendary ECW. When ECW shut its doors, video distributor RF Video needed a new top seller for its wrestling catalog. RF Video owner Rob Feinstein first tried to sign CZW, but when that failed, he created his own.

Now owned by Sinclair Broadcasting, Ring of Honor enjoys the financial resources of its parent company while retaining the flavor of an independent promotion. Sinclair gives Ring of Honor exposure and a budget most independents only dream of, and they use it to draw in the very best wrestlers on the circuit. Ring of Honor served as the launching pad for the careers of many WWE and TNA stars including A.J. Styles, Samoa Joe, Daniel Bryan, Seth Rollins, and Cesaro.

Combat Zone Wrestling owes its existence to ECW as well. After ECW folded, John Danzig opened the promotion in New Jersey to fill the void for fans craving hardcore, violent wrestling. After ten years Danzig sold the promotion to DJ Hyde, who expanded CZW include a wider range of wrestling styles much like ECW in its heyday. The deathmatches are still a major part of the action, largely because they draw so well, but some outstanding wrestlers like Adam Cole have come from Hyde's group. CZW is also the only indie promotion based in the States running shows under their own name overseas.

CHIKARA is easily the most unusual promotion running today. Founded in 2002, CHIKARA grew out of The Wrestle Factory, a wrestling school founded in Allentown, Pennsylvania by Mike Quackenbush and Reckless Youth. CM Punk, Chris Hero, Cesaro, Dean Ambrose, Sara Del Rey, and Colt Cabana are just a few of the stars who have worked for Quackenbush over the years. CHIKARA is known for its high flyers, tag team action, a sense of humor, and innovative storytelling, as detailed in the next chapter.

Dragon Gate USA was founded as an offshoot of Dragon Gate, giving the Japanese promotion an American platform to showcase its roster alongside American talent. In 2011 Dragon Gate USA merged with another independent promotion, Evolve. The two still promote events under their own names but share rosters and even stables of wrestlers. Dean Ambrose and Daniel Bryan are two WWE stars who worked for Dragon Gate USA on their way up.

On the West Coast, the hottest promotion going is Pro Wrestling Guerrilla, an independent founded and run by wrestlers. Like Ring of Honor, PWG is an all-star federation featuring the best of the best from all across the country. Building a strong following for any sport in Los Angeles no small feat, but in the last decade, PWG established a very loyal following in a building as dear to its fans as the ECW Arena. Past stars include Daniel Bryan, Sami Zayn, A.J. Styles, Colt Cabana, Samoa Joe, and Christopher Daniels. Shortly after I began work on this book, PWG celebrated the signing of Kevin Steen by WWE.

Wrestling has become a side gig for celebrities as well. In early 2014 Jeff Jarrett left TNA and announced he was partnering with Toby Keith to start a new promotion called Global Force Wrestling. Billy Corgan of the Smashing Pumpkins started his own promotion Resistance Pro Wrestling in Chicago back in 2011. Resistance Pro is currently shooting a reality TV series, featuring, among others, Mickie Knuckles, "Crazy" Mary Dobson, and Mad Man Pondo.

Mixed in with the regional promotions who fill a void geographically for those who want to watch live wrestling are a number of promotions who fill a different kind of void. As the Hispanic population in the United States has grown, the demand for Lucha Libre has grown with it. Lucha fans can get their fill online and on cable watching Mexican promotions like AAA and Super X Grand Prix. Many of the top AAA stars can be seen on Lucha Underground, an American Lucha Libre production produced by reality TV guru Mark Burnett on Robert Rodriguez's El Rey cable network.

In 2005 Dave Prazak saw an opportunity to fill a similar void. "Working as a manager, I feuded a lot with valets," says Prazak. "Most of the valets were female wrestlers who couldn't get booked as wrestlers. Ian Rotten asked me to start booking women for a women's division at IWA Mid-South."

After taking the IWA Mid-South women's division as far as it could go, Prazak partnered with Ring of Honor to create Shimmer, an all-women's promotion. Prazak booked future WWE Divas Natalia Neidhart and Beth Phoenix on early shows, along with TNA and international phenomenon Awesome Kong. The bookings proved mutually beneficial for Shimmer and the ladies, putting Shimmer at the forefront of a wave of women's promotions like Femme Fatale and Women Superstars Uncensored.

Nearly a decade after they started, Shimmer's crowds are still modest in size, but they've found a huge audience in the video market, distributing shows through Clickwrestle.com. "There's a little bit of beauty in that you can have a tiny show filmed in the middle of nowhere, and people can be watching and experiencing that all over the globe," says Prazak.

As recently as the turn of the century, VHS tape was the preferred format for wrestling fans who wanted to see what was going on in other parts of the country. Thanks to DVD and now digital video, the market for independent wrestling videos has exploded.

Wrestling fans in the Midwest may not be able to get to a PWG show on the West Coast, but they can watch PWG and other regional promotions with the click of a mouse thanks to companies like Highspots and Smart Mark Video.

Founded in 1998 by Mike Burns, Smart Mark Video was created as a distributor for VHS tapes for Future Wrestling Alliance. When FWA folded, Smart Mark Video carried on, offering its services to other promotions. They now offer DVD and video on demand products for CHIKARA, IWA Mid-South, CZW, and many more.

True wrestling fans know that nothing can top the live wrestling experience. Once you've whet your appetite for independent wrestling, it's time to find out what wrestling is happening in your neighborhood. Even if you're not fortunate enough to be in the region of a CZW, PWG, or Ring of Honor, you can find great wrestling at a promotion or school near you. Smaller territories like Ohio Valley Wrestling in Louisville have also earned their reputations by the quality of show and the quality of talent. OVW in particular has been successful at creating stars that went on to bigger things, and Danny Davis is proud to point out that more than 60 people who started in his beginners classes made it to the WWE.

Even the most backwards, backyard wrestling groups can be a pleasant surprise, and you never know where the next big thing will first step into the ring. The old videos of the Trampoline Wrestling Federation that ran shows in North Carolina in the late 90s are laughable - until you realize that's teenage Matt Hardy, Jeff Hardy, Shane Helms, and Shannon Moore taking bumps on the trampoline in the Hardys' backyard.

Indy wrestling also gives fans a good chance to see the stars of days gone by. They may not be able to move and fly like they used to, but you can still find stars like Tommy Dreamer, Sabu, Tracy Smothers, Tito Santana, Nikolai Volkoff, Shane Helms, Ricky Morton, and Bill Dundee doing smaller shows for smaller promotions. It gives the fans a chance to see their old favorites, and it gives the old dogs a chance to give the rub to the stars of the future.

The best thing to do, should you decide to give indie wrestling a chance, is to do a little homework. Find out who the promoter is. Find out if they have a TV show and set your DVR to record an episode. Look at the names and faces on the fliers and do a few Google searches. It's easier than ever to find indie wrestling on video, thanks to YouTube, and many promotions have videos posted online.

You can also learn a lot by looking on Facebook and Twitter. Most indie promoters and wrestlers use social media as their main source of marketing. Social media allows them to connect with fans better than they ever have in the past, and it really gives young wrestlers a vehicle to promote themselves to the fans and the promoters scouting new talent.

Colt Cabana may have given the best advice on indie federations when he spoke about the one that gave him his big break, IWA Mid-South. "Don't buy a ticket online. Don't buy in advance. Go to the arena the day of the show, and if the show's still on, buy a ticket. You will not be disappointed."

The modern day territories are full of hungry wrestlers eager to fill seats so they can follow their dreams. Do a little research and then go out and see a show. Buy t-shirts. Buy videos. Follow, friend, and like the people you enjoy most in the squared circle. Support indie wrestling every way you can. Keep the traditions alive!

Ophidian the Cobra at CHIKARA Pro Wrestling.
(Photo courtesy Ichiban Drunk.)

MAKING IT REAL AGAIN

Professional wrestling is not immune to the corporate takeovers that happen in just about every other business. Several years ago, CHIKARA Pro Wrestling was purchased by the Worldwide Media Development (WMD), a subsidiary of the Titor Conglomerate. The Titor Conglomerate was owned by the Vavasseur family, who also owned a private army, Condor Security.

Conrad Vavasseur, the patriarch of the family, appointed his son Wink as the "Director of Fun" at CHIKARA. Wink did not endear himself to the fans, making many decisions that were not popular. But the issues with Wink quickly became secondary to the rumors that began swirling around the Titor Conglomerate.

A representative from the blog No Private Army gave some highly confidential information to Mike Quackenbush, co-founder of CHIKARA. The package contained information that the Titor Conglomerate had connections to a Nazi religious organization.

The information about Titor was revealed during the June 2, 2013 pay-per-view Aniversario: Never Compromise. As soon as the information went public, the entire CHIKARA locker room was tossed out of the building, save for those involved in the main event. Wink Vavasseur let the main event begin, but the match was never finished. Wink shut down the show and the promotion. Members of Condor Security, another subsidiary of Titor, flooded the arena, striking the set and shooing away the fans. CHIKARA was closed, and all future shows were canceled.

Fans were baffled. Inquiries sent to Quackenbush and other CHIKARA leaders were greeted with silence. A press release stated that all the assets of CHIKARA, including the ring, would be going up for sale. Fans had no choice but to believe the unthinkable had happened: big business had destroyed the renegade promotion they loved.

The entire Titor saga, from the purchase of CHIKARA to the live broadcast shutdown, was reported on multiple wrestling news sites who, like the fans, had no choice but to believe this was for real. In truth, the shutdown was part of a story Mike Quackenbush had worked for years to sell.

Transmedia is defined as telling a story across multiple media platforms, most notably in the digital realm. One of the earliest and most successful examples of this type of storytelling is The Blair Witch Project. The creators of the movie promoted the film as being real. They created a website and second film, a "documentary," to sell this myth. The small budget film became a multi-million dollar hit, and transmedia became the new wave in marketing film and other products.

Through the Titor saga, Mike Quackenbush demonstrated how transmedia could bring some of the suspension of disbelief back to pro wrestling. Quackenbush describes himself as more of a storyteller than a promoter. He was so determined to sell the story to his fans, he actually shut down his own company for nine months.

"My inspiration came from television series *Rubicon* and *The X-Files*, as well as the paranoia/conspiracy thrillers from the 1970s like *The Parallax View* and *Three Days of the Condor*," says Quackenbush. "I like the slower-paced dramas, and especially in the case of Rubicon, you never really know who is pulling the strings, or what their exact motive is. Each piece of that puzzle is a slow reveal that really makes you pay rapt attention to details. I wanted to take some of the most compelling concepts from those works and filter them through the lens of Alan Moore's *Watchmen*, which is a very dense, dark piece that imbues the reader with an all-encompassing sense of dread. All of that takes time. You can't microwave that stuff if you really want it to resonate with the audience, and that is the goal, of course. To take them on an emotional journey, even if sometimes that journey explores an emotional spectrum typically eschewed by professional wrestling."

The seeds of this story were sewn years before the shut down, and CHIKARA spared no expense selling the story. Before news of the buyout broke, CHIKARA created websites for Titor and its subsidiaries. They also set up a toll free number for fans that might try to contact CHIKARA's parent company.

"Pieces of the story needed to be put in place years before they were needed," says Quackenbush. "A bit of foreshadowing. The arrival of a key character. An essential part of the story dropped into our continuing narrative. A lot of that work was done several years in advance."

When CHIKARA went under, the real story began to unfold. In the months following the shutdown, fans began to receive messages and see signs that the wrestlers of CHIKARA were planning to strike back. Fans were sent on a scavenger hunt in Philadelphia to find secret documents exposing the evil actions of the Titor Conglomerate.

Fans also received and spread a coded message found on an eBay auction. Those who decoded the message gathered in Franklin Delano Roosevelt Park, where they discovered the CHIKARA ring was set up. They were treated to an underground show, the first CHIKARA show in months!

Twelve fans also received visitors at their door. Condor Security sent representatives out to interrogate those loyal CHIKARA fans and make sure they were not assisting in the illegal actions of the CHIKARA crew.

The story continued to unfold through real life events, Internet posts, and video. Finally, in May of 2014 the Titor Conglomerate was vanquished and CHIKARA rose from the dead. Monthly shows resumed, and CHIKARA began spinning it's next grand tale.

Although *Pro Wrestling Insider* and other major wrestling sites speculated that the entire shutdown was a work, no one knew for sure until Mike Quackenbush confirmed it on Colt Cabana's podcast. What he and CHIKARA pulled off in 2013 and 2014 was nothing short of revolutionary.

"There were some fans that loved it," says Quackenbush. "They saw in the story the real potential for storytelling that pro-wrestling has at its disposal. They saw how tirelessly we were working to bring something utterly different to an art form that has changed very little in the last few decades. And there were some that did not like it very much at all."

It took years to create the mythology behind the Titor Conglomerate storyline. It took time and money to create and maintain the websites and the social media accounts for Titor. WWE is known to drop angles and change storylines on the fly, and such long range planning, while not unheard of, rarely happens at WWE any more.

It also took the full cooperation of a locker room that understood selling this story meant they would not be working at CHIKARA for a long time! All of the wrestlers had to not only sign non-disclosure agreements, but abide by them to keep any secrets they knew from getting out. Fans saw the tears in the eyes of a referee and heard the sadness in the voices of "fired" stars and had no choice to believe. It's a tribute to the leadership and the talents' belief in those leaders that they were able to keep the lid on the story for so long. Wrestlers aren't exactly famous for keeping secrets, especially in this era.

WWE would never shut itself down for nine months just to sell a story. Neither would TNA or Ring of Honor. All three promotions have parent companies and/or investors to please, and no investor is going to approve removing your primary product from the market for the better part of a year.

CHIKARA isn't owned by a conglomerate. It's owned by its creators, men who are not motivated solely by money. "If money was my purpose, I would have quit or changed what I do after season two," says Quackenbush, who is now on his fourteenth season. He admits that every year, his accountant advises him to close shop because of how little he and the organization make. Mike's purpose is to tell stories and to give the audience back the illusion that wrestling is still real.

It is a rare feat when a wrestler or a promotion can give the fans that feeling in this day and age. CM Punk did it for a night in the summer of 2011 with his pipebomb promo. CHIKARA made their fans believe for the better part of a year. What's more, they made the fans part of the story. It was fans who discovered the secrets Titor was hiding, and it was fans who ultimately saved CHIKARA.

It's hard to say what CHIKARA will do for an encore, or who will follow suit or what, if anything, WWE might do to copy their success. CHIKARA gave their fans a great ride and reason to believe. For a true fan, there is no better gift a promotion can give you.

Chris Hero stares down Reed Bentley.
(Photo courtesy Ichiban Drunk.)

NEVER GIVE UP

Being a professional wrestler today is hard. It's a life of bumps, bruises and breaks. It's a daily grind in the gym, on the road, and at home. It's worrying about bills, wondering if the water will get cut off, and praying that you'll have the money to make it to the next town. When you consider all the obstacles and hardships these people face, you can't help but ask, "Why in the world don't you just quit and get a real job??" Here are your answers in their own words:

Aaron Williams
  I love this business, and I want to be the best.

Austin WGS Bradley
  When my fiancé passed away, I nearly quit the business. I was crushed, and I really wanted to at least take a break. Dave Crist was there when I needed him, and he told me I needed to keep going. He told me to remember why I got into this in the in the first place. I think back to when I used to play with my wrestling figures in my grandparents' basement, and I remember why I love this business. I keep going because I know if I quit now, I will look back and regret it when I am older.

"Crazy" Mary Dobson
  I'm still young! I just got into the business, and I'm only just beginning!

Lylah Lodge
  The thing that keeps me going is the encouragement I get from other people, from my family, fans, and peers. When people see potential in me,

especially when I don't see it myself, it really encourages me.

DJ Hyde

I keep going because this is what I live for. You're miserable every day all week. Then Saturday night comes, and for fifteen minutes, you're truly alive. I do this because I enjoy seeing my guys succeed. More than that, I do this because I have to. I can't do anything else.

Eric Emanon

We all have an expiration date. Mine isn't anytime soon. I will continue to do this until it's not fun anymore. And I don't see that happening for a very, very long time. It's in my blood and in my heart. I love my wrestling family, my brothers in the Indy Card Mafia as well as my brothers and sisters in this business! Without them, there is no me."

Hy Zaya

When I was a kid watching Hogan, I always loved when he Hulked out. He'd get those eyes and start shaking his arms, and the crowd ate it up. It wasn't until I developed a following of my own that I realized that 'Hulk out' moment meant something to the wrestler as well. There's a spirit, an energy that you feed off. It really pumps you up.

Jamin Olivencia

What keeps me going is the enormous amount of support I receive during or after a performance. Good or bad. Affecting people is the greatest gift to my own life purpose.

LuFisto

Sometimes I think that after sacrificing so much for 17 years, after battling injuries and illness and coming back stronger, getting from 200 pounds to what I am now, something amazing must happen. Someone somewhere will give me a chance to shine on a bigger stage. Then reality kicks in. I was close to signing with three different major promotions over the years but something always happened just before and everything got cancelled for various reasons.

I think about the TNA Gut Check disaster where every time I was at the top of the poll, suddenly they would cancel the voting and start over. I think about how many times I was told that I am so good but not pretty enough. I don't have the "Sable aura." I am told I produce quality matches where I make all my opponents look like a million bucks, yet I go to bed feeling like a failure because it seems that for the big companies, I just don't exist. And then, I want to quit.

But then, I show up at a show even if I don't feel like it, go to the ring, wrestle, and the love comes back. I haven't found anything that comes even close to the feeling of going out there and wrestling, pushing your limits, hearing people cheering and giving you a standing ovation for your hard work. I meet the fans, talk to them, and respond to their e-mails.

I don't have any siblings so the boys and girls backstage are my brothers and sisters. Most of them understand my pain, my joy. I don't have children so all the young rookies are like my own that I want to protect and help. I am so proud when my two students, Volkano and Hudson Envy, call me to tell me how good they did in their latest matches, how hard they are working out in the gym.

It is really a love/ hate relationship at this point. I love wrestling but I also hate it. I just hope I can stop before I become bitter about something that brought me so much.

Mad Man Pondo

This is all I know how to do. What else would I do?

Marc Hauss

I am doing this because I love it and I know that I am carving a place for myself in this great sport.

Mickie Knuckles

I wanted to quit after my daughter was born, but decided that until I finish college and can start on that career, this is extra money for my kids for right now. That and a wrestler never truly quits, it is in our blood.

Mitchell Huff, The Chosen One

What motivates me is how much I missed it when I walked away from it. I always regretted not sticking with it, but I'm still young enough to do it. After my first night back in a ring after seven years, my friends and family said they heard a passion in my voice. They could tell I loved it. I always have and always will. I still watch Monday Night Raw every Monday. I just love pro wrestling!

Ron Mathis

I love what I do. I can't see myself doing anything else.

Tyson Dux

Why am I still doing this? I ask myself that question every Monday when I crawl out of bed. I love it, plain and simple. I am addicted to it. It has been my obsession for twenty years. I love every part of it. Being on the road. The other wrestlers who are all my brothers. The fans who appreciate and love it more than I do. My son who loves it and who I would hope I could clear a better path for him if I could.

Mike Quackenbush

Professional wrestling is performance art. I think it's the most fascinating performance art on the planet. It has a limitless potential for storytelling, if we can just embrace the weird fictional space that is uniquely ours. Making wrestling is like making a comic book come to life. It's like opening a doorway and allowing the content of your imagination to pour out onto the stage. That excites me. That keeps me going. Not the dollars and cents of it.

Zodiak

I don't have any plans of quitting any time soon. I have been in this business since 1998, and I still love it to this day. I'm still doing it because I have goals to accomplish and I enjoy developing and teaching other people. Eventually I would love to have or help run a school and do development and production. What motivates me to keep going is I still have that love and passion for what I'm doing. I know who I am and what I want to be. When you know that you really don't feel like you are WORKING but LIVING your life. I also still have a lot to accomplish and see, and I've always tried to avoid being a quitter. I haven't succeeded at that every time for sure, but I keep learning and trying.

Long story short, professional wrestlers are not going away, not as long as there's a ring and someone willing to put them in that ring. That's very good news for those of us who can't get enough of it. So long as fans keep packing the gyms, the warehouses, the roller rinks, and other makeshift "arenas," the sport of professional wrestling will go on. It doesn't matter if the crowd is five thousand or fourteen; they will come, and they will give you their very best.

Every year hundreds of dreamers take the first step to becoming a professional wrestler. Many will quit on the first day. Very few will make it to their first match. Those who make it through are not always the most talented. It takes passion and heart to become a professional wrestler. It takes a willingness to sacrifice and the strength to fight through pain. It takes a steadfast refusal to give up no matter how hard things may become. That's a lesson any dreamer, no matter what their dream, should take to heart.

Next time you see a flier in a store window, take a moment to stop and look. Buy a ticket, cheer your head off, and by all means, please buy something at the tables. One of the young guys on that flier might very well be a future WWE champion, but right now, he could use a little gas money.

ACKNOWLEDGEMENTS

This book would not have been possible without assistance from the men and women of independent wrestling as well as their fans and others who support what they do.

Thank you first and foremost to those who shared their stories with me directly. They are, in no particular order, Jamin Olivencia, Hy Zaya, Delilah Lodge, Austin Bradley, "The Chosen One" Mitchell Huff, Jerrod Harris, Reed Bentley, Aaron Williams, Ron Mathis, Mad Man Pondo, "Crazy" Mary Dobson, LuFisto, DJ Hyde, Mike Quackenbush, Mickie Knuckles, Tyson Dux, Marc Hauss, Eric Emanon, Apollo "Showtime" Garvin, "The Blackanese Assassin" Menace, "Mr. Mo-licious" T.J. Moreschi, Rick Brady, "Crybaby" Chris Alexander, and Zodiak. I strongly encourage any readers interested in learning more about these men and women to look them up on Twitter or Facebook and connect with them.

Thank you to Mike Simpson and Adam Jordan of Marked Out Photography for not only assisting with some of the contacts but providing many of the photos in this book and designing the front cover.

Thank you to all of the other photo contributors, including Ichiban Drunk, Michael Herm of Michael Herm Photography, Sean Ubel of Ubel Photography, Eric Sallotolo, Lylah Lodge, Eric Emanon, Jamin Olivencia, and Tyson Dux.

Thank you to Nick Glenn for the first hand account of the Old Man Charlie story.

Thank you to Vic Filpot for putting together one of the most comprehensive lists of deathmatches you'll ever see in print.

Thank you to Colt Cabana, whose podcast *Art of Wrestling* enabled me to include the stories of many more wrestlers, including himself. Thank you, too, to the guys behind the Ringbelles Women of Wrestling podcast and Steve Austin. They're all on iTunes, and I listen to Colt and Steve every week. Check them out!

Thank you to Evolution Pro Wrestling and IWA Mid-South for their support of this book and *Bluegrass Brawlers*.

Thank you to Michael Ewing, Rick Brady, Ron Aslam, and Destination One Wrestling their support, and for giving me access to their training classes and events. An extra thank you goes to Michael Ewing for proofreading the book not once, but twice.

Thank you to Rich Jones and Bobby Fulton for their support.

Thank you to Randy Pease, who is partly responsible for me becoming a wrestling writer.

Thank you to Kenny Bolin and Jim Cornette for their continued encouragement and support.

Finally, thank you to my wife Jessica for tolerating my mania and encouraging me to keep writing. I love you!

BIBLIOGRAPHY

PODCASTS

Art of Wrestling with Colt Cabana
Episode 45: Tyson Dux, June 2, 2011
Episode 51: Chris Hero, July 14, 2011
Episode 60: Mike Quackenbush, September 15, 2011
Episode 101: Adam Cole, June 28, 2012
Episode 134: Doug Williams, February 14, 2013
Episode 201: Ian Rotten, May 29, 2014
Episode 204: Rip Rogers, June 19, 2014
Episode 215: Cherry Bomb, September 11, 2014
Episode 220: Dave Prazak, October 16, 2014

The Steve Austin Show, Podcast One.
Colt Cabana, October 15, 2013.
Big Van Vader, aka Leon White, May 27, 2014.
Ricky Morton, August 5, 2014.

Women of Wrestling Podcast.
Episode 56: LuFisto, May 13, 2013

ONLINE

Keel, Eli. "Iraq War vet and amputee Michael Hayes doesn't just play the hero for Ohio Valley Wrestling." insiderlouisville.com, June 28, 2013.

LaBar, Justin. "Hero Release by WWE an Attention Grabber." triblive.com, November 10, 2013.

Morales, Vince. "Rebirth of CHIKARA and Its Many Questions." olewrestling.com, February 9, 2014.

VIDEO:

Twist of Fate: The Matt Hardy Story. WWE Home Video.

When Hero Met Punk. IWA Mid-South. Smart Mark Video.

ABOUT THE AUTHOR

John Cosper is the author of *Bluegrass Brawlers: The Story of Professional Wrestling in Louisville.* He is an award winning screenwriter and sketch writer with dozens of short films, several sci-fi novels, and hundreds of sketches to his credit. He lives in the indie wrestling hot bed of Southern Indiana, surrounded by promotions like OVW, D1W, IWA Mid-South, EPW, UWA, CCW, WCCW, Rockstar Pro Wrestling, and SWE. When he's not writing or watching wrestling he's having fun with his wife Jessica and two kids.

The book is over.

Go out and catch a wrestling show.

Now.

Made in the USA
Middletown, DE
18 December 2014